# Contributions to Finance and Accounting

The book series 'Contributions to Finance and Accounting' features the latest research from research areas like financial management, investment, capital markets, financial institutions, FinTech and financial innovation, accounting methods and standards, reporting, and corporate governance, among others. Books published in this series are primarily monographs and edited volumes that present new research results, both theoretical and empirical, on a clearly defined topic. All books are published in print and digital formats and disseminated globally.

Stefano Gatti • Carlo Chiarella • Vitaliano Fiorillo
Editors

# Agriculture as an Alternative Investment

## The Status Quo and Future Perspectives

Springer

*Editors*
Stefano Gatti
ANTIN IP Professor of Infrastructure Finance, Department of Finance
Bocconi University
Milan, Italy

Carlo Chiarella
Department of Finance and Accounting
CUNEF Universidad
Madrid, Spain

Vitaliano Fiorillo
AGRI Lab, SDA Bocconi School of Management
Bocconi University
Milan, Italy

ISSN 2730-6038 ISSN 2730-6046 (electronic)
Contributions to Finance and Accounting
ISBN 978-3-031-27917-1 ISBN 978-3-031-27918-8 (eBook)
https://doi.org/10.1007/978-3-031-27918-8



This Springer imprint is published by the registered company Springer Nature Switzerland AG
The registered company address is: Gewerbestrasse 11, 6330 Cham, Switzerland

# Foreword

As we write, ministers are wrapping up the 27th Conference of the Parties to the United Nations Framework Convention on Climate Change (COP 27), where they launched the first comprehensive global plan to rally both state and non-state actors behind a shared set of adaptation actions, with mandatory implementation by the end of this decade across five impact systems: food and agriculture, water and nature, coastal and oceans, human settlements, and infrastructure. Importantly, this agenda calls for climate-resilient, sustainable agriculture to increase yields by 17% and to cut farm-level greenhouse gas emissions by 21%, without expanding the agricultural frontier. Additional items on the agenda were smart, efficient water systems to reduce water loss and sustainable irrigation systems to preserve water availability while supporting yield growth.[1]

Professor Gatti's latest book, therefore, could not come at a better time to offer thought-provoking insight into agritech as an emerging segment within the infrastructure asset class, a subject that should inspire us all to consider what possibilities can turn into reality and how we can move society toward a more sustainable future.

Throughout history, technological advancement and societal change have been the drivers of innovation, and political will coupled with public and private investment have been the enablers of that change. Infrastructure has always played a central role in transforming that innovation into progress for society. The last decade has seen a wave of new sub-sectors become vital infrastructure, with technological advancements and societal forces blurring the lines between traditional infrastructure verticals. Fiber and telecom towers are examples of assets not necessarily viewed as critical infrastructure 15 years ago, but which now can be recognized as key parts of the infrastructure landscape.

At Antin, we believe that this trend will accelerate, as the current speed of innovation and technological breakthroughs is extraordinary. We are entering a period of significant transformation, powered by new technologies as well as

[1] https://cop27.eg/#/news/197/COP27%20Presidency%20launches%20Shar

forward-looking societal trends and consumer choices that are propagating a new wave of disruption and innovation across all areas of society, including infrastructure. We are focusing closely on these developments as investors and are grateful to be partnered with Bocconi and Professor Gatti's important academic work in these areas.

Professor Gatti's latest research shows that agritech is truly a next-generation sector with the potential to reshape the future of infrastructure. Today, world food security faces challenges on both the demand and supply side. As populations expand with a growing middle class, food demand is increasing exponentially while supply is simultaneously becoming more constrained as urbanization depletes the agricultural workforce and the quality of farmland continues to degrade. Rising protein consumption makes these problems even more acute, given the extreme impact that protein production has traditionally had on the environment and climate. In addition, the war in Ukraine has also underscored the fragility of food supply chains. Beyond these demand and supply side factors, the agriculture industry also faces a unique set of sustainability and climate change issues. The next generation of agriculture infrastructure will be key to changing the trajectory of the industry.

The solutions presented in the book largely focus on boosting efficiency—producing more with less—whether in terms of space, time, or physical resources; enhancing existing food production methods; or introducing new techniques, such as insect-based proteins and closed-loop animal farms. This is why the research undertaken by Professor Gatti and his team is so useful to us at Antin. We have sponsored the Antin IP Associate Professorship in Infrastructure Finance headed by Professor Gatti since 2018 and benefit greatly from his academic research.

We hope you will also benefit from the insightful and thought-provoking findings in this publication.

Antin Infrastructure Partners,
Paris/London, France/UK
December 2022

Alain Rauscher
Mark Crosbie

# Foreword

What is more essential than agriculture? Can a civilization even develop without strong agriculture? Intuition says no. If infrastructure is what transforms innovation into progress, allowing societies and economies to grow, common sense dictates that agriculture is, naturally, *prima inter pares* among primary sectors.

However, it has not historically been considered so. Why is this? What would change this?

There are myriad ways to characterize and define infrastructure, the easiest being a finite group of sectors—a method adopted by many. But at Antin, we believe this is a misguided approach that crucially omits opportunities which display all the characteristics associated with infrastructure but, for various reasons, have not been traditionally viewed as such. More importantly, this very static vision is quickly losing relevance in the context of today's dynamic, rapidly evolving world, as infrastructure is continuously being defined and re-defined.

For these reasons, we identify infrastructure according to a set of five criteria: (1) an essential service; (2) high barriers to entry; (3) stable and recurring cash flows; (4) inflation linkage; and (5) downside protection. At Antin, we believe that an opportunity, whether it be a sector or a business, that ticks these five boxes can be considered infrastructure.

So how does agriculture fit into this matrix? Clearly, it is an essential service: without sustenance, we humans cannot survive. Of the four remaining criteria, stable and recurring cash flows is the one that presents the biggest challenge. Agricultural production is largely cyclical and weather-dependent, resulting in unpredictability and high variance in yields, which ultimately generate price volatility. No farmer can make firm commitments on the quantity or quality of a harvest in one year's time, let alone ten. And in today's world of growing disruption due to climate change, the drivers of yield and price volatility are only intensifying: storms, wildfires, and natural disasters are all ramping up the stress on environmental resources, especially when it comes to arable land and water.

Is this fatal? Is agriculture, despite so obviously being essential for survival, forever uninvestable as an infrastructure sector?

We certainly do not think so. Times are changing: a new "green revolution" is dawning, fostered by agritech, and the transformation will be profound. The megatrends exacerbating the need for change will be explained in Chap. 1, and in Chap. 2, the emerging trends of the green revolution will be described.

Thanks to the emerging trends of the green revolution, opportunities are springing up to leverage new technologies and ideas to better address the needs and aspirations of modern society. The infrastructure of the green revolution requires investment that shares the same emergent philosophy, the ambition for transformation, and last but not least, the long-term vision. Such infrastructure needs patient, visionary capital that brings a new investment approach. All this is presented in Chap. 3, so let me just highlight two of them here.

Let us take weather dependency: controlled environment agriculture can overcome it. This umbrella term covers a broad range of solutions from sophisticated greenhouses to vertical farms, where everything from lighting to temperature to atmospheric chemical composition is monitored and adjusted to ideal growing conditions. In such an optimized environment, crops are neither weather nor season dependent. The fine-tuning of agriculture even in such controlled conditions is easier said than done! But once the sector is stabilized, there is little reason why long-term offtake agreements could not follow, paving the way for stable and recurring cash flows, further facilitating infrastructure investment.

As another example, there is also a whole set of enabling technologies that could become infrastructure, once widely adopted: consider networks of sensors, hybrids of hardware and software, that could help improve pest control distribution, mitigating both health and environmental impacts of pesticides while boosting efficacy, or alternatively, the sophisticated equipment under development today aimed at micro managing irrigation, which potentially reduces water consumption by several factors, thereby optimizing water resources, which are increasingly scarce. All of these technologies, once firmly established, could be the infrastructure of tomorrow—resulting in a transformed agriculture sector.

We have not even touched yet on the production process itself. Much could be said about new proteins and synthetic biology that will revolutionize the products of agriculture.

The possibilities are endless and exciting times are ahead! Change is under way and accelerating, and we are confident that the role of infrastructure investment in agriculture will only continue to grow in the years to come.

Antin Infrastructure Partners,
New York, NY, USA
December 2022

Nathalie Kosciusko-Morizet

# Introduction

Living conditions on our planet are becoming increasingly inhospitable because of climate change. Specifically, the Mediterranean basin and, in particular, Italy and Spain are more and more subject to risks of floods and storms, rising sea levels, water stress, extreme heat waves, and wildfires. As a result, agriculture is called to play a fundamental role in the next few decades not only for the economy but also for individuals. A severe reduction of arable land and available water requires the implementation of processes, techniques, and innovations that can increase productivity and make better use of scarce resources.

This also represents an opportunity for agriculture to emerge as an investment segment in the alternative assets space in the face of the world's food challenges and the risks related to climate change—specifically physical and transition risks. Indeed, investors and asset managers have already started looking at agriculture as an interesting investment theme, as the sector has critical consequences for the planet. What's more, agriculture by nature is characterized by significant externalities and is strongly linked to ESG issues.

At the end of 2021, as far as assets under management (AuM), unlisted agriculture assets have soared more than fourfold since 2012, from about $10 billion to more than $40 billion in 2021 according to the most recent data by Preqin (2022). The quadrupling of AuM has been accompanied by an accumulation of dry powder which has almost doubled since 2012, from $4.6 to $8.6 billion.

Against this backdrop, understanding the future of agriculture is of paramount importance, indispensable for guaranteeing a sustainable future for our planet and the welfare of the world's population. Enhancing our knowledge of this asset class is one imperative step we can take toward reaching this crucial goal.

This book presents the collected results of the fourth year of activity in a five-year research plan to study the future of infrastructure and how to prepare for the unexpected. This work is being carried out by a group of Bocconi University researchers under the Antin IP Associate Professorship in Infrastructure Finance. The goal is to improve and disseminate the culture of infrastructure among academics, professionals, and policymakers, to spark debate on the future of infrastructure and the evolution of how financial markets will support relative investments and financing needs.

Therefore, the book adopts the viewpoint of investors and asset managers in the infrastructure space who have abandoned the overly-simplified sectorial view of infrastructure in favor of an alternative definition based on the key attributes of the investment—assets providing essential services, offering downside protection, stable cash flows, and possibly hedged against inflation. There are very good reasons for this definition of infrastructure to include agriculture:

- *Growing demand and changing dietary preferences*: The expected growth of the world's population to 9.8 billion people in 2050,[2] a rise in the average income (from €8,100 in 2012 to €13,500 in 2050), and ongoing urbanization will determine a surge in food demand and changes in the dietary preferences of many countries.
- *Climate change and resource scarcity*: In technical terms, the ecological footprint of humankind is currently 1.7 times larger than the Earth's biocapacity. In pragmatic terms, as we stand now, that means we need 1.7 Earths to sustain the global population. Agrifood systems account for 31% of the greenhouse gas emissions (GHG) derived from human activities. Agriculture occupies 40% of the world's land and accounts for 70% of water use. (As a side note, water demand is expected to surge by 26% from 2020 to 2050, with more frequent supply shortages concentrated in specific parts of the globe.) At the same time, farmers are increasingly affected by climate change, water and land scarcity, and reduced crop quality. Investors seem aware of the resource scarcity issue. In fact, about 60% of them surveyed by Preqin (2021) see water management and natural disasters/climate change as the most relevant issues for ESG investing.
- *Integration of global trade and the new geopolitical order*: In the context of the rising demand for food and the scarcity of water and arable land, trade has a key role to play. On the one hand, import and export flows may counterbalance an insufficient domestic food supply, which might be due to limited natural resources or supply chain disruptions. On the other hand, however, recent geopolitical tensions could redesign and reset what years of globalization have made possible in the last decades.
- *Technological innovation and digitalization processes*: Technology has the potential to drive up yields 30% by improving process efficiency and minimizing the environmental footprint. This could pave the way to innovative business models along the entire agrifood value chain.

These megatrends have a direct impact on the agriculture value chain, but they also pose fundamental questions about the long-term changes that the sector will experience in the next few years, and how investors can adapt their strategies to the new investment environment. A clear conception of all this is a key success factor for lasting, sustainable investment strategies. Knowledge is essential for long-term

[2] Source: UN Population Division https://www.un.org/development/desa/pd/

investors to identify the best investment opportunities available and to avoid the trap of investing in stranded assets.

To this end, the book collects a series of contributions organized in four chapters, covering first the key megatrends and the investable applications that are expected to reshape the agriculture value chain, and then the implications for infrastructure investors and asset managers.

More specifically, the first chapter, by Vitaliano Fiorillo, Marianna Lo Zoppo, and Aristea Saputo, introduces megatrends with the objective of pinpointing the key challenges for the sector and the innovation underway using PESTLE methodology. More specifically, the chapter starts with an overview of the political, economic, social, technological, legal, or environmental forces that are crucial to the agribusiness sector and details the major challenges deriving from them.

While there is a clear understanding that long-anticipated global changes are now taking place at a faster-than-expected rate, scholars and practitioners in any industry are trying to understand how the winds will change by analyzing megatrends. The discussion about megatrends has been going on for more than a decade now, but the outcome of the academic work attempting to identify and interpret individual megatrends often failed to understand interactions among them that could scale up or down their positive or negative effects. Different sources depict only partially overlapping scenarios, emphasizing alternative perspectives on the role of each megatrend.

In the first chapter, the authors compile the final shortlist of 26 megatrends that will be shaping industries at least until 2030–2040. Crucially, since megatrends can gain and lose strength over time, depending on the interactions with other similar phenomena, the analysis specifically extends to ascertain the most crucial global forces of change with a systematic analysis of interdependencies.

More in detail, mutually strengthening and mitigating interactions are considered, as deduced from the existing literature and empirical observation. The result is a list of nine key major phenomena defined as global driving forces of change: emerging economies; expanding globalization; aging of the global population; population growth slowdown and peak; middle-class expansion in developing countries and changing consumption patterns; increasing data ubiquity; rising groundbreaking technologies; climate change; and depletion of natural resources and ecosystem services. These key driving forces are expected to shape the future and dramatically change the basic needs of society, first of all as regards the way food and energy are produced, but also relating to the need to drastically and quickly reduce the environmental impact of this production. The change in basic needs suggests that humanity may face alternative development paths that require us to design a strategy to overcome these challenges and proactively support this strategy through large investments.

Among all the impacts that the driving forces listed above may have on several industries, agribusiness in particular is directly or indirectly facing the largest number of challenges: the growing demand for food, feed, fibers and energy, changing dietary preferences, climate change, natural resources scarcity, technological advancements and integration of global trade—all this is striking the industry faster and harder than expected. These multiple and interacting challenges for agribusiness suggest that a radical paradigm shift is in order, such as the need to increase productivity while cutting environmental impacts, to make more efficient use of natural resources, to enhance ecosystem services, to reduce food waste and loss, to improve public nutrition and health, and to achieve a better distribution of value along the supply chain.

Against this backdrop, the chapter then moves on to discuss the technological innovations emerging along the entire agribusiness value chain that might contribute to tackling the industry challenges mentioned above. In particular, the authors show that because of the key role it plays in ensuring future prosperity combined with the pressure it is exposed to, agribusiness is a lively field for innovation. Innovative farming systems, advances in chemistry and biotechnology, renewable energies, technological tools to enhance efficiency along the entire supply chain, alternative sources of protein, and the incorporation of cross-industry technologies and applications: these are the main innovation trajectories in the industry, resulting in a wide array of investment opportunities.

The second chapter, by Vitaliano Fiorillo, Marianna Lo Zoppo, and Aristea Saputo, further concentrates on the 8 trends, 22 applications, and 47 technologies emerging from Chap. 1. With a mix of desk analysis and structured interviews, the authors examine both the technical aspects and the external factors that can influence the diffusion of these innovations and their success as business concepts, including social legitimacy and regulatory support. The goal is to identify a subset of promising investable applications and to map them in terms of potential interest for each player in the agribusiness supply chain.

More specifically, in Chap. 2 the authors address the dual question: What innovations in agribusiness will be the key to overcoming the challenges and making investments profitable?

To answer the question, they narrow down the analysis to the most relevant ones, ranging from biotechnology to renewable energy, from alternative proteins and novel farming systems to traceability technologies and digital marketplaces. The goal is to understand which of innovations have the highest potential to respond to the challenges posed by the key driving forces.

It is not uncommon to witness a concentration of investments in early-stage technologies which are wiped out in a bubble burst. So to clearly understand the potential, the analysis digs deep while taking multiple perspectives. There might be promising technological innovations that hardly ever win the favor of stakeholders and bog down investors in unprofitable investments and ineffective solutions. On the other hand, some early-stage technologies might ramp up quickly and solve multiple issues at once. Recently, in terms of the interest in the industry that has attracted more than $40 billion according to Preqin (2022), the hype over technological innovation has raised expectations, but the risk of bubbles is still very high. This is mainly because, however fascinating technologies may appear to be, the truth lies in a comprehensive, sustainable approach.

To clear away the generalized technology-hype and reveal the most promising areas for investors, the analysis considers both the stage of technical and business development, on the one hand, and the level of acceptance and legitimacy that innovations receive from the market and stakeholders, on the other. The first dimension captures the technological risk embedded in the proposed applications, while the latter outlines the potential regulatory or societal red flags that may undermine their investment case.

Chapter 3, by Stefano Gatti and Carlo Chiarella, looks instead at the intersection of agriculture and infrastructure investments to investigate prospects for investors and asset managers with a long-term horizon, such as those investing in infrastructure, to embrace a theme-based investing approach focused on agritech. The chapter starts with an overview of the status quo of agriculture investment, providing first a description of the specific features characterizing the asset class, then introducing a taxonomy of investors, and finally commenting on recent trends in fundraising and investments. Then, attention turns to the agritech-focused private equity and venture capital space and studies its overlap with the infrastructure asset class in terms of the investor base, asset management industry, and investment opportunity set, with the aim of drawing out specific implications for investors and asset managers.

Agribusiness has become more and more interesting not only for venture capitalists and private equity investors but also for more conservative infrastructure investors and asset managers in search of stable, inflation-linked returns, resilient to downturns and not correlated with other asset classes. In other words, as agribusiness proves to be a key industry in overcoming global challenges, what truly makes it an alternative asset class, conceptually, is that investments could turn any investor into an "impact investor" with a positive net return on the balance between humanity's needs and natural capital. Looking at innovations along the agribusiness supply chain, investor appetite seems to support this ideal concept, concentrating on four main areas: improving agricultural productivity, minimizing food loss and reducing waste; conserving natural capital and enhancing ecosystem services; improving public nutrition and health; and distributing value along the supply chain more effectively.

Chapter 4 summarizes the main results from each contribution and sheds light on directions for future research in this field. What was once the objective of scattered, disarticulated sustainability programs in single companies, institutions, NGOs, and research centers is now the focus of structured, largely funded, widespread R&D programs, with ever-challenging objectives. If a considerable part of the innovations taking place along the agribusiness supply chain succeeded, humanity could actually face a paradigm shift in multiple aspects of the global economy. Ultimately, the world would be able to achieve most of the United Nations' Sustainable Development Goals by 2050.

ANTIN IP Professor of Infrastructure Finance, Bocconi University, Milan, Italy — Stefano Gatti
AGRI Lab, SDA Bocconi School of Management, Milan, Italy — Vitaliano Fiorillo
CUNEF Universidad, Madrid, Spain — Carlo Chiarella

## References

Preqin 2022 Global Natural Resources Report. https://www.preqin.com/insights/global-reports/2022-preqin-global-natural-resources-report
UN Population Division https://www.un.org/development/desa/pd/

# Contents


**1 Megatrends Affecting Agribusiness: From Challenges to Opportunities** . . . . . 1
Vitaliano Fiorillo, Marianna Lo Zoppo, and Aristea Saputo
1.1 Introduction . . . . . 1
1.2 An Overview of Megatrends . . . . . 4
1.2.1 Identifying Key Megatrends . . . . . 4
1.2.2 What Will Affect Business in the Next Five to Ten Years? . . . . . 5
1.2.3 Megatrends in the PESTLE Analysis . . . . . 7
1.2.4 The Driving Forces . . . . . 8
1.3 Megatrends and Challenges in the Agribusiness Industry . . . . . 13
1.3.1 Delving into Megatrends and Challenges in Agribusiness . . . . . 13
1.3.2 Agribusiness Megatrends . . . . . 14
1.3.3 Agribusiness Industry Challenges . . . . . 17
1.4 Innovation Trajectories in the Agribusiness Sector . . . . . 20
1.4.1 Spotting Agribusiness Technological Innovations . . . . . 20
1.4.2 Renewable Energy in Agriculture . . . . . 24
1.4.3 Chemistry and Biotechnology . . . . . 26
1.4.4 Novel Farming Systems . . . . . 28
1.4.5 Innovative Aquaculture . . . . . 30
1.4.6 Agritech . . . . . 31
1.4.7 Alternative Proteins . . . . . 32
1.4.8 Food Safety and Traceability . . . . . 34
1.4.9 E-commerce . . . . . 36
1.5 Conclusion . . . . . 37
References . . . . . 38
Megatrends Analysis: Literary Sources . . . . . 38
Agribusiness Megatrends and Challenges Analysis Literary Sources . . . . . 39

Technological Innovations Analysis Literary Sources . . . . . . . . . . 39
Other References . . . . . . . . . . . . . . . . . . . . . . . . . . . . . . 41

**2 Innovation Trends in the Agribusiness Supply Chain** . . . . . . . . . . . . 45
Vitaliano Fiorillo, Marianna Lo Zoppo, and Aristea Saputo
2.1 Introduction . . . . . . . . . . . . . . . . . . . . . . . . . . . . . . . . 45
2.2 The Agribusiness Innovation Landscape: Who Is Innovating and Why? . . . . . . . . . . . . . . . . . . . . . . . . . . . . . . . . . . 47
2.2.1 Dissecting Technological Innovations in the Agribusiness Industry . . . . . . . . . . . . . . . . . . . . . . . . . . . 47
2.2.2 Distribution of Technological Innovations Along the Supply Chain . . . . . . . . . . . . . . . . . . . . . . . . . . . 48
2.2.3 Matching Innovations and Industry Challenges . . . . . . . . . 58
2.3 Technical and Business Development of Agribusiness Innovations and Implications for Investors . . . . . . . . . . . . . . . . . . 60
2.3.1 Assessing the Potential of Technological Innovations . . . . . 60
2.3.2 The Status of Technological Innovations in the Industry . . . 62
2.3.3 Looking Forward: Perspectives Ten Years from Now . . . . . 68
2.4 Conclusion . . . . . . . . . . . . . . . . . . . . . . . . . . . . . . . . . 71
References . . . . . . . . . . . . . . . . . . . . . . . . . . . . . . . . . . . 71

**3 Agriculture as an Asset Class in the Alternative Investments Space** . . . . . . . . . . . . . . . . . . . . . . . . . . . . . . . . 73
Stefano Gatti and Carlo Chiarella
3.1 Introduction . . . . . . . . . . . . . . . . . . . . . . . . . . . . . . . . 73
3.2 Agriculture Investing . . . . . . . . . . . . . . . . . . . . . . . . . . . 75
3.2.1 Agriculture as an Asset Class . . . . . . . . . . . . . . . . . . . . 76
3.2.2 A Taxonomy of Agriculture Investors . . . . . . . . . . . . . . . 78
3.2.3 A Map of Fundraising and Investment in the Agriculture Asset Class . . . . . . . . . . . . . . . . . . . . . . . . . . . . . . . 80
3.3 Can Agriculture Become an Asset Class in the Infrastructure Space? . . . . . . . . . . . . . . . . . . . . . . . . . . . . . . . . . . . 82
3.3.1 The Status Quo at the Intersection Between Agriculture and Infrastructure Asset Classes . . . . . . . . . . . 82
3.4 Conclusion . . . . . . . . . . . . . . . . . . . . . . . . . . . . . . . . . 97
References . . . . . . . . . . . . . . . . . . . . . . . . . . . . . . . . . . . 98

**Conclusions** . . . . . . . . . . . . . . . . . . . . . . . . . . . . . . . . . . . 101

# Chapter 1
# Megatrends Affecting Agribusiness: From Challenges to Opportunities

**Vitaliano Fiorillo, Marianna Lo Zoppo, and Aristea Saputo**

## 1.1 Introduction

Agribusiness is a relatively recent word, first used in the late 1950s in the USA. At that time, the term referred to "the sum of all farming operations, plus the manufacture and distribution of farm commodities" (Davis, 1995). While this first definition put farms at the center, over time they have become part of complex and articulated supply chains made up of many players operating globally. The definition of agribusiness has thus been expanded to include all commercial and management activities carried out by companies that (I) provide inputs to the agricultural sector; (II) transform, transport, and distribute agricultural products; and (III) finance the sector (Downey & Erickson, 1987).

To date, the companies operating in the agribusiness supply chain differ widely in terms of size, business models, and technological level, characterized by equally heterogeneous competitive dynamics. To simplify the interpretation of the industry, we can identify six levels in the value chain (see Fig. 1.1). Upstream there are providers of services, technology, and inputs (e.g., agrochemicals, fertilizers, seeds) that sell their products and services to farms, which in turn use them to produce raw materials. In the midstream, wholesalers and intermediaries collect large quantities of produce from several farms and sell it to industrial manufacturers. The latter process raw materials to transform them into finished products such as food, feed, clothing, and fuels, as well as many other industrial and consumer products. Downstream in the supply chain, distributors (supermarket chains, the hotel-restaurant-catering channel (Ho.Re.Ca), and retailers) sell finished products to final consumers and delivery services.

V. Fiorillo (✉) · M. Lo Zoppo · A. Saputo
AGRI Lab, SDA Bocconi School of Management, Milan, Italy
e-mail: vitaliano.fiorillo@sdabocconi.it; marianna.lozoppo@sdabocconi.it; aristea.saputo@sdabocconi.it



S. Gatti et al. (eds.), *Agriculture as an Alternative Investment*, Contributions to Finance and Accounting, https://doi.org/10.1007/978-3-031-27918-8_1

**Fig. 1.1** The agribusiness supply chain (Source: AGRI Lab)

Supply chain processes are inherently complex across industries, with multiple functions interacting with different potentially conflicting objectives and several dependencies between material and information flows. The agricultural supply chain is further complicated by operational factors such as poorly predictable yields and external factors (such as weather conditions), input availability, farmers' capabilities, and price volatility arising from global imbalances in supply and demand and/or geopolitical instability. Finally, the characteristics and competitive dynamics of a multitude of players drive innovation and value creation differently along the chain.

To truly understand the complexity of this supply chain we need to take a step back and look at the changes that have characterized the world food system from the "Green Revolution"[1] onward. In the past few decades, each player in the value chain has followed a distinctive evolution. Upstream in the supply chain, input providers have undergone a significant concentration over the years: today a few companies dominate the global market.[2] The same trend has characterized distribution companies; a series of vertical and horizontal mergers and acquisitions among the main brands have reduced the market to a few dozen traders (KPMG International, 2013).

At the manufacturing stage, complex transformation processes have proliferated significantly, adding value to raw materials: to date, consumers can choose from an ever-expanding, more personalized range of products. To summarize, input providers, manufacturers, and distributors evolved following the dynamics of industrialization first and servitization more recently.[3] The growth of these companies was made possible, above all, by their ability to understand the market and create value for their customers.

[1]The term "Green Revolution," first used in 1968 by William S. Gaud, administrator at the United States Agency for International Development, commonly refers to the period from 1965 to 1980. At this time, high-yielding crop varieties, starting from rice, wheat, and maize developments (Griffin, 1979) and related technologies and policies were exported to Asia and Latin America through international research institutes and donor networks (Brooks, 2005). This process was triggered to find a technological solution to the so-called Malthusian catastrophe, namely the moment when the population (exponential growth) outpaces the food supply increase (linear growth), causing famines, wars, and depopulation (Goodman & Redclift, 1991).

[2]Even though concentration varies across countries and product categories, the global seed, crop protection chemicals, and biotechnology market are currently dominated almost entirely by four companies. Historically, Monsanto, Bayer, BASF, Syngenta, Dow, and DuPont were once the "Big Six," but recent mergers, driven by the portfolio complementarity of some of these players, have reduced their number to four (Bayer-Monsanto, DowDuPont/Corteva, ChemChina-Syngenta, BASF) (Deconinck, 2020)

[3]The term refers to firms adding services to their offering as a means of increasing competitiveness, turnover, and market power (Vandermerwe & Rada, 1988).

At the primary production level, the main trends in recent decades have been the intensification of agriculture, the growing control and use of inputs such as fertilizers and agrochemicals, and the increase in the average size of large companies, as opposed to a growing fragmentation of smaller, marginalized ones. Compared to other players in the value chain, farms did not follow an equally rapid or profitable development path, becoming potentially the weakest link in the chain.

If, on the one hand, the transition to the current food system has undeniably ensured greater food security in some parts of the planet, thanks to augmented yields (Gladek et al., 2017) and the expansion of cultivated areas, on the other hand, it is now facing major challenges. Indeed, there seems to be clear agreement on the need for a paradigm shift (Global Panel on Agriculture and Food Systems for Nutrition, 2016). In particular, four divergent arguments support this hypothesis:

1. Today's food system is unable to feed the growing population (Foley et al., 2011; West et al., 2014).
2. The global food system can provide enough caloric intake to feed the world's population but only in quantitative and not qualitative terms: the real challenge is to guarantee nutritional quality (Haddad et al., 2016).
3. The distribution of the quantity and value of what is produced (in terms of volumes and calories) is uneven across regions and society. Here the focus is on the apparent paradox that although overall, current food systems are producing enough food to feed the world's population, nearly one billion people still experience starvation (Dixon et al., 2007).
4. The activities of the food system hurt the environment. Some data may be useful to frame the extent of the phenomenon which seems to be the most urgent challenge: agriculture occupies about half of the planet's arable land (FAO, 2015), while a thousand years ago this figure was only 4% (Ritchie & Roser, 2013); agriculture uses 69% of the freshwater extracted (Aquastat, 2014); together with the rest of the food chain, agriculture is responsible for almost 30% of greenhouse gas emissions and 75% of deforestation globally (IPCC, 2014).

Lastly, the food system is exposed to global forces of change, defined as megatrends, affecting humanity as a whole and the agribusiness industry in particular. These forces include, for example, the growing demand for food, feed, fibers, and energy, changing dietary preferences, climate change, natural resource scarcity, technological advancements, and integration of global trade. Megatrends represent multiple, interacting challenges for agribusiness, such as the necessity to increase productivity while cutting environmental impacts, to make more efficient use of natural resources and enhance ecosystem services, to reduce food waste and losses, to improve public nutrition and health, and to achieve a better distribution of value along the supply chain.

Because of its key role in ensuring future prosperity, agribusiness is a lively field for innovation. Innovative farming systems, advances in chemistry and biotechnology, renewable energies, technological tools to boost efficiency along the entire supply chain, alternative sources of proteins, and the incorporation of cross-industry technologies and applications: these are the main innovation trajectories in the industry, resulting in a wide array of investment opportunities.

Against this backdrop, it shouldn't be surprising that agriculture is also capturing the attention of investors. And this is true not only for venture capitalists and private equity but also for more conservative infrastructure investors and asset managers in search of stable, inflation-linked returns that are resilient to downturns and not correlated with other asset classes, as discussed in Chap. 3.

In this chapter, we outline the current global megatrends, the challenges influencing the agribusiness industry, and a map of the industry's main technological innovations. More precisely, in Sect. 1.2, we offer an overview of the megatrends that are exerting a force of change on businesses across industries, categorizing them as political, economic, social, technological, legal, or environmental, and investigate their mutually reinforcing or mitigating effects, identifying the most influential ones, which we define as "driving forces." Then in Sect. 1.3, we narrow down the list to highlight the megatrends that are crucial to the agribusiness sector and to identify the major challenges deriving from them. To conclude, in Sect. 1.4, we introduce an overall picture of the technological innovations emerging along the agribusiness value chain that might contribute to tackling the industry challenges mentioned above.

## 1.2 An Overview of Megatrends

### *1.2.1 Identifying Key Megatrends*

Given the intricacy of world dynamics, providing an overview of the megatrends affecting businesses is a complex task if not pursued on the basis of a robust methodology. First, while the international literature is filled with valuable analyses of the forces of change that exert pressure on industrial activities, not all of them can be labeled as megatrends. The latter are to be distinguished from other phenomena according to a set of specific features. They are forces of social, economic, political, technological, and environmental change (Naisbitt & Aburdene, 1990; Hajkowicz, 2015) that occur globally and that have the potential to influence the basic functioning of society as a whole and to condition the developmental trajectories of humankind (Pęciak, 2016) over a long interval of time. This period is usually set at seven to ten years at least (Naisbitt & Aburdene, 1990; Hajkowicz, 2015). Moreover, different sources depict only partially overlapping scenarios, emphasizing alternative outlooks on the role of each megatrend.

In this publication, we have derived a final shortlist of 26 megatrends shaping industries at least until 2030–2040 (hereinafter megatrends), selecting them based on how often they are mentioned in the literature we examined, building on a thorough review of academic papers and publications from public institutions, non-governmental organizations (NGOs), non-profit organizations (NPOs), consulting and investment companies. We also considered their influence according to a sample of academic experts that we surveyed, asking them to rate each identified megatrend depending on the significance of its impact.

While relevant per se, any megatrend can gain or lose strength over time, depending on its interactions with other similar phenomena. Therefore, identifying the most crucial global forces of change requires a systematic analysis of such interdependencies. To do so, we slotted the megatrends we identified into a cross-impact matrix aimed at assessing the influence of each one on the others to pinpoint the "driving forces," meaning the megatrends that exert an influence on an above-average number of other global phenomena. We considered both mutually strengthening and mitigating interactions, as deduced from the existing literature and empirical observation.

As a result, we found nine megatrends that qualify as driving forces: growing economies of emerging countries; increasing economic connectedness across borders (i.e., globalization); the aging of the global population; population growth slowdown and peak; middle-class expansion in developing countries and changing consumption patterns (i.e., consumerism); escalating data ubiquity; rising technologies (automation, AI, cloud computing, biotechnologies); climate change (e.g., higher temperatures, the melting Arctic, extreme weather events, sea level rise, natural disasters); and the depletion of natural resources and ecosystem services.

### 1.2.2 *What Will Affect Business in the Next Five to Ten Years?*

The combination of the literature review and the survey resulted in a shortlist of 26 megatrends that will affect the business world in its entirety in the next five to ten years, regardless of the industry. Table 1.1 includes all the megatrends that emerged from the literature review and clusters them into the PESTLE analysis dimensions (i.e., politics, economics, society, technology, law, and environment).[4] In addition, it reports for each megatrend the factors used as criteria for the final selection, namely the frequency of mentions in the reviewed literature and the percentage of business experts who consider the megatrend's impact as relevant. More specifically, the analysis excluded megatrends that were mentioned less than ten times in the examined literature (i.e., below-average mentions) and deemed relevant in terms of impact by fewer than half of the business experts in our sample.

In **bold** are the megatrends that were included in the final shortlist.

[4]PESTLE is the acronymic for politics, economics, society, technology, law, and environment. PESTLE analysis is a theoretical framework that businesses can adopt to assess the external factors that (may) affect the context in which they are operating or in which they plan to launch new operations, and adapt their strategy accordingly (Aguilar, 1967).

**Table 1.1** Megatrends

| Category | Megatrend | Literature mentions | Relevant for % of experts |
|---|---|---|---|
| Politics | Establishment of a multipolar world with changes in international relationships (i.e., rise of Asia) | 4 | 12.5% |
| | **Exacerbating international tensions and conflicts (e.g., connected to resource scarcity, climate change, and new energy sources)** | 16 | 25% |
| | **Emergence of new arenas of state competition** | 15 | 12.5% |
| | **Stalling of convergence around shared values (e.g., human rights, etc.), and populism and protectionism derived from polarization** | 18 | 12.5% |
| | **Weakening multilateralism in favor of ad hoc organizations** | 15 | 12.5% |
| Economics | **Growing economies of emerging countries** | 16 | 25% |
| | Fragmentation of the trading environment | 3 | 37.5% |
| | Expanding knowledge-based economy and service economy leading to industries disruption | 3 | 37.5% |
| | Space economy development | 1 | 12.5% |
| | **Increasing economic connectedness across borders** | 10 | 12.5% |
| | Rising national debts | 2 | 12.5% |
| | Continuing "winner-take-all" multinationals and State-owned companies' impact on global competition | 2 | 25% |
| Society | **Aging global population** | 22 | 87.5% |
| | **Population growth slowdown and peak** | 18 | 50% |
| | **Middle-class expansion in developing countries and changing consumption patterns (i.e., consumerism)** | 12 | 50% |
| | **Continuing urbanization** | 22 | 37.5% |
| | **Increasing migrations** | 18 | 62.5% |
| | **Growing (economic, technological, social) inequality within and across countries** | 19 | 62.5% |
| Technology | **Changing jobs connected to new technologies and data exploitation** | 19 | 87.5% |
| | **Hyperconnectivity in a world of digital natives** | 23 | 62.5% |
| | **Increasing data ubiquity** | 3 | 50% |
| | **Increasing relevance of technologies for sustainability** | 3 | 62.5% |
| | **Rising technologies: automation, AI, cloud computing, biotechnologies** | 26 | 75% |
| | Lowering technology life cycle | 0 | 25% |
| | **Convergence of unrelated areas of scientific research and technological applications** | 1 | 50% |
| Law[a] | **Adapting rules to new technologies** | 1 | 12.5% |
| | **Adapting rules to aging population issues** | 0 | 25% |
| | **Adapting rules to climate change and resource scarcity issues** | 2 | 50% |

(continued)

**Table 1.1** (continued)

| Category | Megatrend | Literature mentions | Relevant for % of experts |
|---|---|---|---|
| | **Increasing relevance of consumer protection laws** | 1 | 12.5% |
| | **Increasing relevance of intellectual property laws** | 1 | 12.5% |
| Environment | **Climate change (e.g., higher temperatures, melting Arctic, extreme weather events, sea level rise, natural disasters)** | 23 | 50% |
| | **Mounting human pressure on the environment** | 17 | 37.5% |
| | **Natural resources and ecosystem services depletion** | 22 | 50% |

Source: AGRI Lab

[a]Concerning selection criteria, an exception was made for legal megatrends. These forces were mentioned by less than ten literature sources, and they were deemed as relevant by less than half of the business experts' sample. This may be because legal megatrends are often activated because of other phenomena. Nonetheless, we still opted to include them to consider every dimension of the PESTLE analysis.

BlackRock (2018); Boumphrey and Brehmer (2018); Deloitte (2017); European Environmental Agency (2018); European Parliament (2017); European Strategy and Policy Analysis System (2015); European Union Commission (2018); EYQ (2018); FAO (2017a); Fornasiero et al. (2021); Forum for the Future (2019); IPSOS (2020); Laudicina et al. (2018); McKinsey & Company (2017); OECD (2016); Office of the Director of National Intelligence (2021); Pano (2019); PWC (2019); Retief et al. (2016); SardÃ and Pogutz (2018); Sydney Business Insights (2019); Trend One (2019); UNDESA (2019); UNDP and UNRISD (2017); Wall (2018); Winston (2019); Z_punkt (2019)

### 1.2.3 Megatrends in the PESTLE Analysis

From a political perspective, resource scarcity will be one of the many factors progressively worsening as a consequence of international tensions and conflicts. Moreover, international convergence around shared values, such as human rights, has characterized the second half of the last century. But this may stall and polarize public opinion, leading to populist and protectionist initiatives, further exacerbating international relations and regional turmoil. As in the past, thanks to technological progress, wars will also evolve and belligerents will explore new arenas for competition (e.g., cyber wars and space wars). At the same time, nations will need to preserve their sovereignty as multilateralism will keep weakening in favor of ad hoc organizations such as regional or purpose-specific alliances.

From an economic point of view, two major globalization trends will keep transforming the world scenario, as they have already done in the past few decades: the growth of emerging economies and the intensified connectedness of economies across borders.

From a social standpoint, in the next decade, the business world will be influenced by six main forces: global population growth; global population aging; middle-class expansion in developing countries; urbanization; increasing migrations; and escalating (economic, technological, and social) inequality within and across countries (Gatti & Chiarella, 2020). More specifically, population growth at a global level will slow down and peak before 2100, with the only exception being in sub-Saharan Africa, where the population is projected to steadily rise, eventually accounting for more than half of the expected global population expansion (UNDESA, 2019a). At the same time, the aging trend will continue, affecting developing countries (possibly before they reach the income level of high-income countries) at a faster pace than developed ones, where the process started in the middle of the last century. Although the middle class in emerging economies will expand, inequalities within and across countries will persist and keep widening in several domains, from income disparities to social discrimination and the technological divide. Finally, urban areas will continue to swell, with intensifying migration flows, and about 68% of the global population living in cities by 2050 (UNDESA, 2019b).

As for technological development, here conceived as the exponential growth in quantity and sophistication of the technological tools at the service of human activities inside and outside of the economy, this will play a major role in our future as innovations will be more and more pervasive across every domain of our lives. Indeed, future generations of digital natives (i.e., people born in contexts pervaded by the presence of technologies) will live in a "hyper-connected" world, in which new jobs will emerge as a response to new technologies and masses of data will continue to be collected and analyzed (Credit Suisse, 2017). The academic sources we reviewed emphasize the relevance of the spread of technologies such as the Internet of Things (IoT), artificial intelligence (AI), cloud computing, and biotechnologies as a crucial step in the transformation of our production and consumption models.

From an environmental standpoint, it is worth underlining that the need for effective responses to the consequences of climate change will be a major booster for the development and deployment of new sustainable technologies. Indeed, the climate crisis, as well as the depletion of resources and ecosystem services, is predicted to be further aggravated because of the mounting human pressure on nature.

In this scenario, legal megatrends will follow, as norms will adapt to the issues raised by the consequences of demographic shifts, technological innovations, and climate change. At the same time, stricter consumer protection laws will be enforced, concerning not only warranties and planned product obsolescence, but also privacy and data security. On the other hand, businesses will increasingly rely on intellectual property rights to escape the commoditization trap, secure their inventions, and manage large-scale open innovation.

### *1.2.4 The Driving Forces*

As mentioned in Sect. 1.2.1, megatrends are interconnected and can either mutually strengthen or mitigate each other. An analysis of their interactions through a cross-impact matrix (reported in Fig. 1.2) allowed us to identify, within the list of

- In **bold**: effects detected through known and proven data in the literature (the remainder are effects detected through empirical assumptions).
- 1: reinforcing effect / -1: mitigating effect

| | | Politics | | | | Economics | | Society | | | | | | Technology | | | | | | Law | | | | | Environment | | |
|---|---|---|---|---|---|---|---|---|---|---|---|---|---|---|---|---|---|---|---|---|---|---|---|---|---|---|---|
| | | Exacerbating international tensions and conflicts (e.g. connected to resource scarcity, climate change and new energy sources) | Emergence of new arenas of state competition | Stalling of convergence around shared values (e.g., human rights etc.), and populism and protectionism derived from polarization | Weakening multilateralism in favor of ad hoc or-ganizations | Growing economies of emerging countries | Increasing economic connectedness across bor-ders (i.e., globalization) | Ageing global population | Population growth slow-down and peak | Middle-class expansion in developing countries and changing consumption patterns (i.e. consumerism) | Continuing urbanization | Increasing migrations | Growing (economic, technological, social) inequal-ity within and across countries | Changing jobs connected to new technologies and data exploitation | Hyper connectivity in a world of digital natives | Increasing data ubiquity | Increasing relevance of technologies for sustainability | Rising technologies: automation, AI, cloud computing, biotechnologies | Convergence of unrelated areas of scientific research and technological applications | Adapting rules to new technologies | Adapting rules to ageing population issues | Adapting rules to climate change and resource scarcity issues | Increasing relevance of consumer protection laws | Increasing relevance of intellectual property laws | Climate change (e.g. higher temperatures, melting Arctic, extreme weather events, sea level rise, natural disasters) | Mounting human pressure on environment | Resources and ecosystems services depletion |
| Politics | Exacerbating international tensions and conflicts (e.g. connected to resource scarcity, climate change and new energy sources) | | | | 1 | | | | | | | 1 | | | | | | | | | | | | | | | |
| | Emergence of new arenas of state competition | 1 | | | | | | | | | | | | | | | | | | | | | | | | | |
| | Stalling of convergence around shared values (e.g., human rights etc.), and populism and protectionism derived from polarization | 1 | | | 1 | | | | | | | | | | | | | | | | | | | | | | |
| | Weakening multilateralism in favor of ad hoc or-ganizations | | | | | | | | | | | | | | | | | | | | | | | | | | |
| Economics | Growing economies of emerging countries | 1 | | 1 | 1 | | | | | 1 | 1 | 1 | | | | | | | | | | | | | | 1 | |
| | Increasing economic connectedness across bor-ders (i.e., globalization) | | 1 | 1 | 1 | 1 | | | | | | | | 1 | | | | | 1 | | | | | | | | |
| Society | Ageing global population | | | | | 1 | | | 1 | 1 | | | 1 | | | | | | | | 1 | | | | | | |
| | Population growth slow-down and peak | | | | | 1 | | 1 | | | 1 | 1 | 1 | | | | | | | | | | | | | 1 | |
| | Middle-class expansion in developing countries and changing consumption patterns (i.e. consumerism) | | | -1 | | 1 | | | 1 | | 1 | 1 | 1 | | | | | | | | | | | | | 1 | |
| | Continuing urbanization | | | | | | | | | | | | | | | | | 1 | | | | | | | | 1 | |
| | Increasing migrations | 1 | | 1 | | | | | | | 1 | | 1 | | | | | | | | | | | | | | |
| | Growing (economic, technological, social) inequal-ity within and across countries | 1 | | 1 | | | | | | | | 1 | | | | | | | | | | | | | | | |

**Fig. 1.2** Cross-impact matrix (Source: AGRI Lab)

| | | Politics | | | | Economics | | Society | | | | | | Technology | | | | | | Law | | | | | Environment | | |
|---|---|---|---|---|---|---|---|---|---|---|---|---|---|---|---|---|---|---|---|---|---|---|---|---|---|---|---|
| | | Exacerbating international tensions and conflicts (e.g. connected to resource scarcity, climate change and new energy sources) | Emergence of new arenas of state competition | Stalling of convergence around shared values (e.g., human rights etc.), and populism and protectionism derived from polarization | Weakening multilateralism in favor of ad hoc or-ganizations | Growing economies of emerging countries | Increasing economic connectedness across bor-ders (i.e., globalization) | Ageing global population | Population growth slow-down and peak | Middle-class expansion in developing countries and changing consumption patterns (i.e. consumerism) | Continuing urbanization | Increasing migrations | Growing (economic, technological, social) inequal-ity within and across countries | Changing jobs connected to new technologies and data exploitation | Hyper connectivity in a world of digital natives | Increasing data ubiquity | Increasing relevance of technologies for sustainability | Rising technologies: automation, AI, cloud computing, biotechnologies | Convergence of unrelated areas of scientific research and technological applications | Adapting rules to new technologies | Adapting rules to ageing population issues | Adapting rules to climate change and resource scarcity issues | Increasing relevance of consumer protection laws | Increasing relevance of intellectual property laws | Climate change (e.g. higher temperatures, melting Arctic, extreme weather events, sea level rise, natural disasters) | Mounting human pressure on environment | Resources and ecosystems services depletion |
| Technology | Changing jobs connected to new technologies and data exploitation | | | 1 | | | | | | | | | 1 | | | | | | | | | | | | | | |
| | Hyper connectivity in a world of digital natives | | | | | | 1 | | | | | | | 1 | | | | | | 1 | | | 1 | | | | |
| | Increasing data ubiquity | | 1 | | | | | | | | | | 1 | 1 | | | | | | 1 | | | 1 | | 1 | -1 | 1 |
| | Increasing relevance of technologies for sustainability | | | | | | | | | | | | | | | | | | | | | | | | | -1 | -1 |
| | Rising technologies: automation, AI, cloud computing, biotechnologies | | 1 | | | 1 | 1 | | | 1 | 1 | | 1 | 1 | 1 | 1 | 1 | | | 1 | | | 1 | 1 | | | |
| | Convergence of unrelated areas of scientific research and technological applications | | | | | | | | | | | | | 1 | | | | 1 | | 1 | | | | | | | |
| Law | Adapting rules to new technologies | 1 | | | | | | | | | | | | | | | | | | | | | 1 | 1 | | | |
| | Adapting rules to ageing population issues | | | | | | | | | | | | | | | | | | | | | | | | | | |
| | Adapting rules to climate change and resource scarcity issues | 1 | | | | | | | | | | | | | | | | | | | | | | | | -1 | -1 |
| | Increasing relevance of consumer protection laws | 1 | | 1 | | | | | | | | | | | | | | | | | | | | | | | |
| | Increasing relevance of intellectual property laws | 1 | | 1 | | | | | | | | | | | | | | | | | | | | | | | |
| Environment | Climate change (e.g. higher temperatures, melting Arctic, extreme weather events, sea level rise, natural disasters) | 1 | 1 | 1 | 1 | 1 | | | | 1 | 1 | 1 | 1 | | | 1 | 1 | | 1 | | | 1 | | | | | 1 |
| | Mounting human pressure on environment | 1 | | | | | | | | | | | | | | | | | | | | 1 | | | 1 | | 1 |
| | Natural resources and ecosystem services depletion | 1 | | 1 | 1 | 1 | | | | 1 | 1 | 1 | 1 | | | 1 | 1 | | 1 | | | 1 | | | 1 | | |

Fig. 1.2 (continued)

megatrends, the "driving forces," namely the forces of change that will influence an above-average number of other global phenomena. Figure 1.2 shows for each megatrend the total number of other megatrends it influences. Driving forces are defined consequently and highlighted in **bold** in Table 1.2.

**Table 1.2** The driving forces as a result of the cross-impact matrix

| Category | Megatrend | No of impacted megatrends |
|---|---|---|
| Politics | Exacerbating international tensions and conflicts (e.g., connected to resource scarcity, climate change, and new energy sources) | 2 |
| | Emergence of new arenas of state competition | 1 |
| | Stalling of convergence around shared values (e.g., human rights, etc.) and populism and protectionism derived from polarization | 2 |
| | Weakening multilateralism in favor of ad hoc organizations | 0 |
| Economics | **Growing economies of emerging countries** | 7 |
| | **Increasing economic connectedness across borders (i.e., globalization)** | 6 |
| Society | **Aging global population** | 5 |
| | **Population growth slow-down and peak** | 6 |
| | **Middle-class expansion in developing countries and changing consumption patterns (i.e., consumerism)** | 7 |
| | Continuing urbanization | 2 |
| | Increasing migrations | 4 |
| | Growing (economic, technological, social) inequality within and across countries | 3 |
| Technology | Changing jobs connected to new technologies and data exploitation | 2 |
| | Hyperconnectivity in a world of digital natives | 4 |
| | **Increasing data ubiquity** | 8 |
| | Increasing relevance of technologies for sustainability | 2 |
| | **Rising technologies: automation, AI, cloud computing, biotechnologies** | 14 |
| | Convergence of unrelated areas of scientific research and technological applications | 3 |
| Law | Adapting rules to new technologies | 3 |
| | Adapting rules to aging population issues | 0 |
| | Adapting rules to climate change and resource scarcity issues | 3 |
| | Increasing relevance of consumer protection laws | 2 |
| | Increasing relevance of intellectual property laws | 2 |
| Environment | **Climate change (e.g., higher temperatures, melting Arctic, extreme weather events, sea level rise, natural disasters)** | 14 |
| | Mounting human pressure on the environment | 4 |
| | **Natural resources and ecosystem services depletion** | 13 |

Source: AGRI Lab

According to the cross-impact matrix results, climate change; the depletion of natural resources and ecosystem services; and technologies such as AI, automation, cloud computing, and biotechnologies will be the most impactful megatrends in the near future, affecting 13 to 14 other global phenomena. The other driving forces exert an influence on five to eight other phenomena and include social megatrends (the global population growth peak and aging, and middle-class expansion accompanied by changing consumption patterns), economic megatrends (the growing economies of emerging countries and the economic connectedness across borders), and one technological megatrend (the centrality of data). These, while mitigated by other ongoing or forthcoming phenomena, will be the most relevant driving forces in the coming years.

Concerning technological development, the massive adoption of interconnected technologies in urban areas may enable more efficient use of resources, mitigate the consequences of natural disasters (CDRI, 2021; CCRI, 2021), and foster inclusion and wellbeing in cities. New technological tools may connect remote areas, potentially reducing the migratory pressure on urban centers. Inside and outside cities, digital natives are experiencing and will continue to explore new forms of sociality, enabled by expanding internet coverage. Similarly, elderly and ill people will be supported through new assistance and distance healthcare tools in hospitals or at home. The job market will also be deeply transformed, as in-demand professions and skills will evolve at the pace of technological discoveries.

At a higher level, the possibility to develop or access new technologies will determine the rise or fall of global economic and political powers; technology access and development will also be crucial in minimizing or amplifying the economic disparities within and across countries and will open new arenas for competition among nations. In addition, new technologies will continue to influence world trade, investment targets, industrial supply chain structure, and consumer habits, strengthening—while transforming—the ongoing process of globalization.

Hopefully, thanks to greater awareness of the global environmental crisis, innovation will also redirect the current trajectories of production and consumption toward a more sustainable future, enabling new resource extraction, manufacturing, and sale and re-use processes, as well as ecosystem service preservation and recovery.

Ongoing radical transformations are already taking place due to climate change and the impoverishment of natural resources and ecosystem services (such as the loss of biodiversity and natural habitats and the disturbance of geochemical cycles due to pollution). In the coming years, the availability of resources and exposure to extreme atmospheric phenomena and natural disasters will influence political and economic balances, determining the future of states and regions based on their vulnerability from an environmental point of view and their readiness to face the climate crisis. The consequences of these forces will affect both rural areas and urban centers. More than likely, already disadvantaged regions will be hit more severely, leading to migratory flows and exacerbating pre-existing economic disparities.

In addition, the identification and application of coordinated strategies to manage resource scarcity and the climate crisis will influence international relations, leaving room for geopolitical tensions, in a context characterized by the misalignment of shared values and the heightening polarization of political positions, supported by the rise of populist and protectionist movements (Hofrichter, 2017). The extraction and allocation of new resources will set the battlefield in the future, as in the case of the race to exploit resources at the poles and outside the Earth's orbit. Changes in the geopolitical balance and widespread distrust among nations may reduce the ability to collectively confront global challenges, and the heightened sense of insecurity derived from a globalized world will also result in the rise of new forms of governance involving public and private actors regardless of states or regional borders.

In Sect. 1.2.3., our analysis highlighted the fundamental role that demographic megatrends, and in particular the growth and aging of the world's population, will play in the coming years. Indeed, any forecast or future strategy needs to factor in two billion additional individuals who will inhabit the planet by 2050, putting additional pressure on available resources. This pressure will be especially intense if accompanied by the expansion of the middle class in developing economies and the spread of the consumerist culture. Nonetheless, most of the sources we examined report a slowdown in population growth and expect it to stabilize and start declining by the end of the century. However, the consequent increment in the average age will have equally destabilizing repercussions, in particular on the economic growth opportunities of nations and their subsistence systems. This will require decision-makers to find more and more resources while rethinking professions, modes of work, and intergenerational solidarity systems.

## 1.3 Megatrends and Challenges in the Agribusiness Industry

### *1.3.1 Delving into Megatrends and Challenges in Agribusiness*

In this section, after the general analysis of the megatrends affecting every business, we delve deeper into the agribusiness industry to identify the global forces of change that are influencing its evolution and the resulting challenges that the sector needs to face. While the described 26 megatrends and 9 driving forces provide an overall picture of the global scenario in which the agribusiness industry is (and will be) operating in the next years, an additional literature review, triangulating multiple academic and non-academic sources (FAO, 2017b, 2018; Kirova et al., 2019; Maggio et al., 2019; OECD/FAO, 2021), revealed the mega-trends that are particularly pertinent to the agribusiness sector (hereinafter "agribusiness mega-trends"), and the main challenges that they will bring along.

## 1.3.2 Agribusiness Megatrends

The analysis showed that 13 out of the 26 listed megatrends are mentioned at least once in the documents we reviewed that specifically discuss future agribusiness scenarios.

As shown in Fig. 1.3, among these, three are cited in all documents as major forces influencing the sector, namely the peak of population growth, the key role of innovation and new emerging technologies, and climate change. Five are reported by at least half of the sources and pertain to changing consumption patterns and diets, the scarcity of natural resources, the integration of international trade (referring both to the increasing connectedness of the world's economies, reverberating on food security goals and international competition, and the uncertainty related to trade agreements and restrictions) (Matthey, 2021), the rise in average income, and urbanization (both mostly mentioned concerning change in dietary habits, partially overlapping with the shift in consumption patterns). On the other hand, five megatrends are reported in less than half of the documents: persistent inequality, the growth of the world economy, an aging global population, and the proliferation of conflicts and migrations.

Notably, even though the latter megatrends are mentioned only by a limited number of sources on agribusiness, they will still exert an influence on the industry. For example, the growth of the world economy will materialize mainly through the rise of the average income and the shift of consumption patterns. Also, the aging of the global population will have a major influence in rural areas, where older farmers will have a harder time facing the consequences of climate change and natural resources depletion, adopting technological innovations and accessing credit or other income-generating mechanisms.

Similarly, current circumstances in Eastern Europe clearly demonstrate how rising conflicts can undermine established trade relations. Interestingly, persistent inequality is mentioned not as a megatrend but as an agribusiness industry challenge, shifting the perspective adopted in the general analysis and pointing to the agribusiness sector as a crucial player in future solutions to these phenomena.

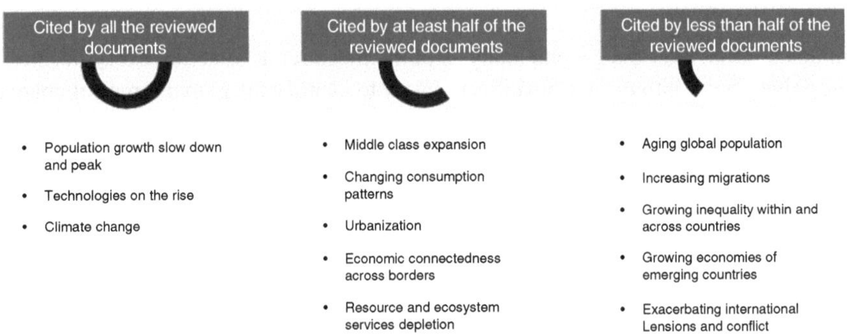


**Fig. 1.3** Megatrends analysis (Source: AGRI Lab)

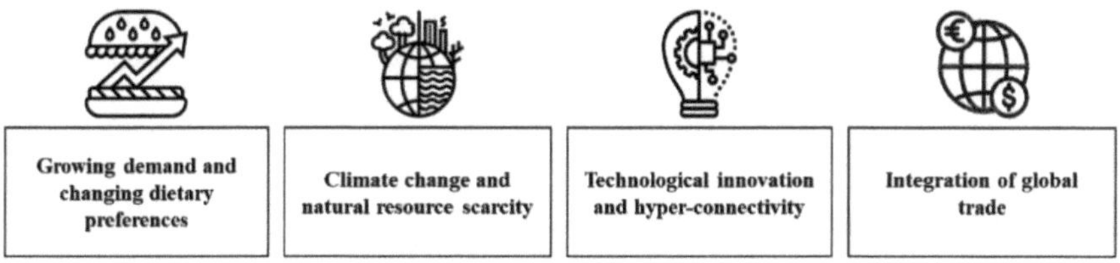


**Fig. 1.4** Agribusiness megatrends (Source: AGRI Lab)

By grouping and renaming megatrends reported by more than half of the reviewed publications, we shed light on the links with agribusiness, as well as the overlap with the driving forces mentioned above, reconfirming the latter's relevance for the future of every industry (see Fig. 1.4):

1. growing demand and changing dietary preferences (which groups together world population growth, rising income at a global level and consumption pattern changes),
2. climate change and natural resource scarcity,
3. technological innovation and hyperconnectivity,
4. integration of global trade.

## Growing Demand and Changing Dietary Preferences

The expected growth of the world population (projected to reach 9.8 billion in 2050) (UNDESA, 2017), and of the average annual GDP per capita (from €8147 in 2012 to €13,503 in 2050) (Kirova et al., 2019), as well as ongoing urbanization, will determine a rise in food demand and changes in the dietary preferences of many countries (FAO, 2018). Developing nations will play a key role, as they will host the greater share of the population and income increase, and their dietary patterns are tending to converge with those of developed countries.

Indeed, developing nations are now showing substantial diet diversification, and they are passing from consuming mainly home-produced food to purchasing market products more frequently (IFAD, 2016). Meat consumption at a global level has surged by 58% from 1998 to 2018, reaching 360 million tons per year (OECD, 2022), and it is expected to double from 2008 to 2050, up to 570 million tons per year (The World Counts, 2022). Interestingly, 54% of the rise in consumption in the last 20 years is due to population increase, while the remaining portion can be traced back to the growth of per capita consumption, with developing countries accounting for 85% of the global increase (OECD, 2022). Moreover, the middle classes of these countries are paying more attention to food safety and quality, in particular with regard to semi-processed and perishable foods (Pingali & Prabhu, 2006). Notably, new dietary preferences deriving from income growth are expected to develop not only among those individuals who change their status from poor to middle class but also among those who move across income segments within the poverty range. Indeed, even the rural poor are already buyers in the global food market (IFAD, 2016).

**Climate Change and Natural Resources Scarcity**

According to FAO, 31% of the total GHG emissions derived from human activities (corresponding to about 16.5 billion tons) are generated by agrifood systems, starting from land use, inputs production, and farming practices to include household consumption and waste disposal (FAO, 2021). Currently, agriculture occupies about 40% of the world's land, with this portion expected to increment by 5% by 2050; agriculture also accounts for 70% of freshwater use (Kirova et al., 2019; Societé Generale Cross Asset Research, 2019). At the same time, farmers are affected more and more by climate change, water, and land scarcity, and diminished quality of crop yields. Droughts and floods are expected to depress yields, and soil erosion and desertification already cause the loss of 19–23 hectares per minute. Notably, tropical regions will be the most affected, reducing food availability and the stability of food supplies for their populations (Kirova et al., 2019).

**Technological Innovation and Hyperconnectivity**

According to a recent publication by the European Commission (Kirova et al., 2019), technological advances could potentially boost agriculture production more than land expansion, determining up to a 30% growth in yields. Indeed, such advances can contribute to enhancing efficiency in the use of resources, for example, enabling innovative water and land conservation techniques, and agricultural processes (as is the case with farm automation). Furthermore, progress in this field can foster the rise of new business models; an example here is e-platforms. Coherently with all other sectors, agriculture will also benefit from enhanced connectivity as a key enabler of technologies such as IoT and analytics applications (Maggio et al., 2019). In addition, mobile phones have great potential in terms of inclusiveness as they can help keep the industry operators informed about innovations, supporting their decision-making processes by supplying data on inputs availability, prices, or weather conditions, and connecting them with their partners along the value chain (FAO, 2017a, 2017b).

Technological developments are not occurring only in agriculture, but across the entire agrifood value chain, starting from inputs producers up to delivery services. All this translates into higher efficiency and a lower environmental burden from these activities, fostering the adoption of innovative production, management, and governance models. However, it is important to note that since R&D investments are mainly concentrated in developed countries, the current paths of adoption and dissemination of technologies may exacerbate the disparities between high-income countries and those with excessive levels of poverty and hunger (FAO, 2017a, 2017b). Although private investments and the lowering of technology costs can help lessen this gap, public interventions will be needed to counterbalance this phenomenon (FAO, 2017a, 2017b).

#### Integration of Global Trade

The increasing demand for food requires a sustainable expansion of the food supply across world regions. Trade has a key role to play here as imports may counterbalance a domestic lack of food due to limited natural resources or episodic natural disasters that can hit agricultural production or disrupt supply chains (FAO, 2017a, 2017b). At the same time, the integration of trade across countries can bring about new employment opportunities in low- and middle-income countries (Kirova et al., 2019). Nonetheless, globalization may also entail entry barriers for small-scale producers and an unfair distribution of value along the supply chain, given by the unrivaled bargaining power of a few big players and the consolidation of distribution channels (Kirova et al., 2019).

### *1.3.3 Agribusiness Industry Challenges*

Building on the arguments in the literature about the agribusiness megatrends, we identified four main challenges for the sector:

- Improvement of agriculture productivity and food loss/waste reduction: In the next few years, an escalation of food demand associated with the deterioration of natural ecosystems will put pressure on agriculture productivity; this will necessitate cutting the current inefficiencies related to food loss and waste that occur at different stages of the chain, largely contingent on more and more sophisticated consumer demands and perceptions.
- Efficient use of natural resources and enhancement of ecosystem services: The deterioration of ecosystems represents a threat to human activities and lives; agriculture is called to use natural resources more efficiently to mitigate its impacts on the environment and to restore and enhance ecosystem services wherever depleted or endangered, often by agribusiness itself.
- Improvement of public nutrition and health: In the face of the current population growth rate and persistent inequalities, the agrifood industry is asked to ensure food security for all and to improve public nutrition and health.
- Better distribution of value along the supply chain: While the integration of global trade can contribute to meeting the above-mentioned challenges, it may also continue threatening the fair distribution of value along the supply chain. In this context, the agribusiness industry must find a new balance for agricultural operators to access the generated added value.

Figure 1.5 reports the challenges that the sector needs to address, showing their links with the megatrends under investigation.

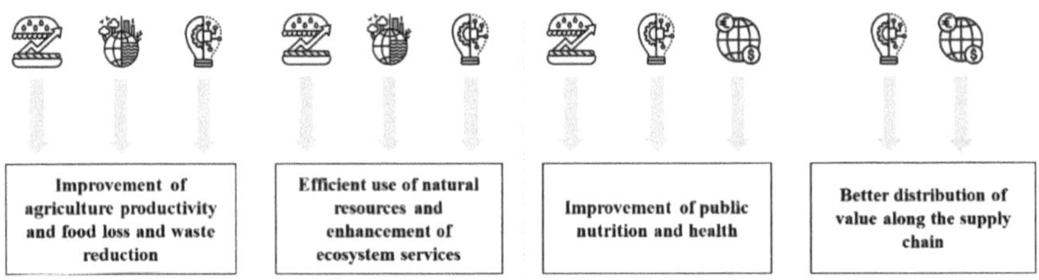


**Fig. 1.5** Agribusiness industry challenges (Source: AGRI Lab)

### Improvement of Agriculture Productivity and Food Loss and Waste Reduction

To respond to the expected rise in food demand and new dietary preferences, a 50% scale-up in food and feed production with respect to 2019 levels is required (Kirova et al., 2019). Although agriculture productivity is currently a vibrant field of research, further innovation is necessary to achieve food security for all, while limiting agriculture's impacts on the environment. For example, the proliferation of livestock farming is considered particularly challenging. In fact, this sector already accounts for almost 80% of all the land devoted to agriculture, if we include both grazing land and croplands earmarked for feed production (Kirova et al., 2019; Ritchie, 2017), and it creates a significant environmental burden.

Once again, it is important to point out that responses to the need to feed a growing population should focus not only on opportunities to increase agriculture productivity, but also on reducing the current degree of food loss and waste, with the former occurring along the supply chain, and the latter referring to food that is fit for consumption but goes to waste at a retail or household level. In fact, about one-third of the food produced globally is not consumed due to major food losses and waste. Notably, the quantity of wasted food is comparable across countries (Kirova et al., 2019), with food loss happening mostly in low- and middle-income countries for several reasons (e.g., sub-optimal farming practices, poor storage, inadequate skill and technologies, inflexible logistics, and inefficient markets) (WWF, 2022); waste in advanced economies instead is mostly due to consumption habits. Other than decreasing the availability of food, waste and loss are also major causes of environmental impacts, linked to the unnecessary use of land, water, energy, agricultural inputs, and GHG emissions derived from both the production of food that is lost and the wasted food itself (WWF, 2022).

### Efficient Use of Resources and Enhancement of Ecosystem Services

The need to use natural resources efficiently represents the backdrop for all the agrifood industry challenges in the near future. Given its key role for human life, agriculture must radically redesign its production and distribution processes and encourage new patterns of consumption. The aim here is not only for this industry to ensure food security for all, but to do so while reducing its footprint on the environment to preserve natural capital.

### Improvement of Public Nutrition and Health

Currently, about 821 million people are undernourished, and each year about 3.5 million people die due to a lack of essential nutrients (FAO, IFAD, UNICEF, WFP, and WHO, 2022). At the same time, obesity has nearly tripled since 1975, and the majority of the global population lives in countries where more people die of obesity or being overweight than undernourishment (WHO, 2021). Beyond producing enough food to feed the world's population, the agrifood system must diminish its imbalances to improve public nutrition and health, downsizing the existing polarization between diets of low- and high-income countries, with the former harshly affected by undernutrition (which concern mostly children and women) and the latter by obesity (which starts earlier and earlier in childhood, with all associated pathologies such as diabetes).

Improved agricultural and manufacturing practices, logistics, infrastructure, storage conditions, and international trade are needed to overcome undernutrition. On the other end of the spectrum, healthier and more sustainable dietary patterns should be encouraged to tackle obesity through improved consumer literacy, education, economic incentives, public norms and self-regulations, promoted by several actors, such as policymakers, agrifood operators, the media, and society as a whole (Kirova et al., 2019; Financial Times, 2022a).

### Better Distribution of Value Along the Supply Chain

Unfair trade practices are allegedly widespread along the agrifood value chain, and they are defined as "grossly deviating from good commercial conduct, contrary to good faith and fair dealing and unilaterally imposed by one trading partner on another" (Fałkowski et al., 2017). This causes an unbalanced distribution of value among the value chain operators. Due to the combined concentration and consolidation in the input, food processing, and distribution industries, the bargaining power of larger multinationals exceeds smaller, individual operators, farms in particular (COPA-COGECA, 2018). In such circumstances, buyer-imposed conditions may diminish suppliers' welfare and result in gains that are retained by intermediaries and not passed on to consumers (Gorton et al., 2017).

Moreover, farmers themselves may be prompted to adopt unfair trade practices, for example reducing the quality of their products to lower their costs (Fałkowski et al., 2017). Indeed, in contexts characterized by unfair trade practices, competitive pressure and industry norms may exacerbate and tighten market conditions, activating additional unfair trade practices (Fałkowski et al., 2017). Notably, such practices are equally present in low- and high-income countries. A survey conducted by Oxfam, in fact, confirmed that 96% of suppliers in the EU food chain have been subjected to unfair trade practices. In the United Kingdom, 52.8% of the consumer price goes to supermarkets, 38.5% to traders and food manufacturers, and only 5.7% to small- scale farmers (Oxfam, 2018). In France, out of €100 spent on food, only €15 returns to farms (COPA-COGECA, 2018).

In light of this, the agrifood industry must reconsider such practices, including shifting unfair risks and costs, and levying charges, making unilateral amendments to contract terms, abrupt and unjustified termination of contracts or commercial relationships (Sexton, 2017).

To meet these challenges—namely, boosting agriculture productivity and handling food loss and waste, using resources efficiently and enhancing ecosystem services, improving public nutrition and health, and stopping unfair distribution along the value chain—the agribusiness industry should transform its prevailing dynamics. In this complex scenario, technological innovations will contribute to the sector's evolution.

## 1.4 Innovation Trajectories in the Agribusiness Sector

### *1.4.1 Spotting Agribusiness Technological Innovations*

While the agribusiness sector is being impacted by megatrends and called to respond to urgent challenges on a global level, technological innovations emerge as valuable a means for implementing new production models all along the industry's value chain, along with other non-tech-based solutions. This section presents the results of a literature review, including academic papers, reports from consulting and investment companies, and publications from NGOs and NPOs. This review aims to explore the technological innovations occurring in the agribusiness sector to spotlight the most promising ones.

More specifically, laying the foundations for the discussion in Chap. 3, the focus is on the innovations in technological processes used in agriculture and farming with the greatest potential to obtain long-term sustainable returns for investors, where the agriculture and infrastructure segments intersect in the alternative assets space.

We identified a vast number of items and present them according to the SDA Bocconi DEVO Lab HIT Radar Taxonomy,[5] which makes a distinction between four main categories: innovation trends and business models, applications, technologies, and building blocks (see Fig. 1.6).

[5]The DEVO Lab is the SDA Bocconi's center of excellence for the study of digital technologies and their implications for companies. The HIT Radar is the tool developed by the DEVO Lab to evaluate the impact, ecosystem, and dynamics of digital technological objects for mid- to large-size enterprises. Within the HIT Radar, the taxonomy classification is the process that allows us to clearly identify and categorize the collected technological objects, to then accurately highlight the relationships between them (Castelli et al., 2022).

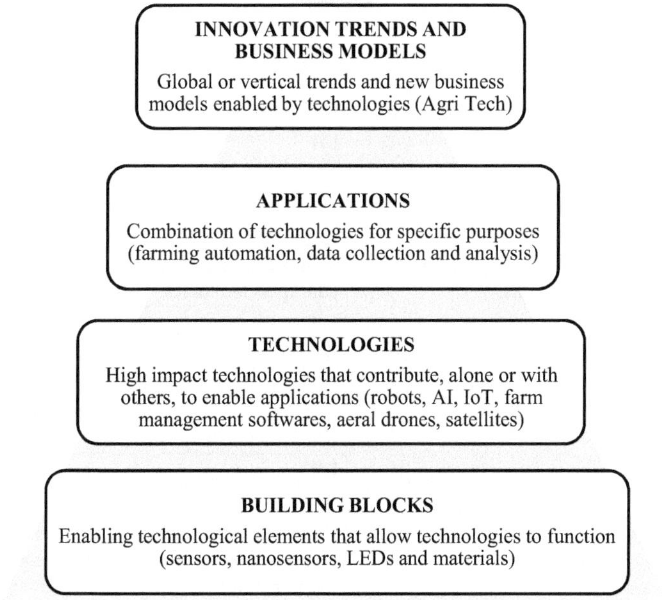


**Fig. 1.6** DEVO Lab HIT Radar Taxonomy (Source: DEVO Lab)

- Innovation trends and business models include global or vertical trajectories of change and new business models enabled by technologies. For example, the term "agritech" does not encompass a single technology, but several different types of technological innovations. However, the development of any technology in this field is driven by the same purpose, which is producing more in less space and/or with fewer inputs, all to boost agricultural efficiency.
- Applications can be defined as combinations of technologies for specific purposes. If agritech is the trend, farming automation and data collection and analysis are applications that make it possible to upgrade the efficiency of agricultural processes.
- Technologies, instead, contribute to application enabling. For example, robots, AI, IoT, farm management software, aerial drones and satellites enable farming automation and data collection and analysis, for example.
- Lastly, building blocks can be defined as individual technological elements that enable technologies to function. This category mainly includes sensors, nanosensors, LEDs, and materials.

As a result of the process described above, 8 innovation trends and business models, 22 applications, and 47 technologies were identified, as reported in Table 1.3. Building blocks instead were only mentioned when considered essential and highly strategic for technology.

**Table 1.3** Map of innovation trends and business models, applications, and technologies (Source: AGRI Lab)

| Trends & business models | Applications | Technologies |
|---|---|---|
| Renewable energy in agriculture | Bioenergy production | Advanced bio-methane |
| | | Hydrogen |
| | Intelligent agrivoltaics | Electricity generation from solar panel |
| | | IoT |
| | | AI |
| | Solar desalination for irrigation | Solar-powered desalination |
| Chemistry and biotechnology | New breeding techniques for plants | Plant DNA sequencing, synthesis, assembly, and editing technologies |
| | | IoT |
| | | AI |
| | New breeding techniques for livestock | Biotechnologies for livestock health, genetics (genomic selection), and reproduction (e.g., artificial insemination) |
| | | IoT |
| | | AI |
| | New breeding techniques for fish | Biotechnologies for fish health, genetics (genomic selection), and reproduction (e.g., artificial insemination) |
| | | IoT |
| | | AI |
| Novel farming systems | Vertical farming | Hydroponic, aeroponic, or aquaponic growing systems |
| | | Lighting systems |
| | | Heating, ventilation, and air conditioning (HVAC) systems |
| | | IoT |
| | | AI |
| | Algae farming | Harvesting from wild stocks (mechanical or by hand) |
| | | Water quality management systems (based on IoT, AI and machine learning—ML) |
| | | Land-based recirculating aquaculture system |
| | Insect farming | Breeding systems (including separation and cleaning rooms) |
| | | Food processing technologies |
| Innovative aquaculture | Land-based aquaculture | Land-based recirculating aquaculture system |
| | | Water quality management systems (based on IoT, AI, and machine learning—ML) |
| | Sea-based aquaculture | Alternative sea farming solutions (e.g., closed or semi-closed facilities at sea, offshore farming) |
| | | Advanced well-boats |
| | Precision aquaculture | IoT |

(continued)

**Table 1.3** (continued)

| Trends & business models | Applications | Technologies |
|---|---|---|
| | | AI |
| | | Computer vision |
| | | Robots |
| Agritech | Fuel efficiency | Hybrid and pure electric vehicles and drones |
| | | Fuel-cell hydrogen vehicles |
| | | Autonomous vehicles (automated steering, supervised autonomy) |
| | | On-board autonomous navigation and controls, on-board diagnostics, and data analytics dashboard |
| | | AI |
| | Farming automation | Precision irrigation technology |
| | | In-field robots |
| | | Post-harvest robots |
| | | Livestock automation |
| | | IoT |
| | | AI |
| | Data collection and analysis | Improved climate forecasts |
| | | Farm management software |
| | | Unmanned aerial vehicles (aerial drones) |
| | | Satellites |
| | | IoT |
| | | AI |
| Alternative proteins | Cultivated meat (including seafood) | Cell-culture media technology (synthetic biology) |
| | | Bio-printing/polymer spinning technologies |
| | Plant-based products | Extrusion technology (to produce Textured Vegetable Protein—TVP) |
| | | Extended shelf-life processes (e.g., heat-pasteurization, high-pressure processing, addition of antimicrobials) |
| | | Bio-printing |
| | Fermentation-derived protein | Selection and/or cell engineering |
| | | Traditional/biomass/precision fermentation bioprocess |
| Food safety and traceability | Smart packaging: active, intelligent, and connected | Absorbent, emitters, and releasers materials and agents |
| | | Chemical, bio-, and edible sensors |
| | | IoT |
| | | AI |
| | Food preservation | Innovative technologies for food preservation (e.g., irradiation, high-pressure technology, pulsed electric field) |

(continued)

**Table 1.3** (continued)

| Trends & business models | Applications | Technologies |
|---|---|---|
| | | Hyperspectral imaging, image analysis, spectroscopy |
| | | AI and machine learning |
| | Smart traceability | Blockchain/Radio-Frequency Identification (RFID) |
| | | IoT |
| | | AI |
| E-commerce | Food delivery ecosystem | Virtual marketplaces |
| | | AI |
| | | Robots for food preparation |
| | | Delivery robots |

Ag Funder (2020); Agrilyst (2016); Ahmad et al. (2021); AlShrouf (2017a); Amit et al. (2017); Antonucci and Costa (2020); Araújo et al. (2021); Ashok et al. (2020); Baiano (2020); Bayer Crop Science Division (2021); Behzadi et al. (2018); Biggs and Giles (2013); Birkby (2016); Daghari and El Zarroug (2020); De Clercq et al. (2018); Dossey et al. (2016); Drago et al. (2020); Duhan et al. (2017); EY (2020); FAO (2000); Five Seasons Ventures (2019); GFI (2020a, 2020b, 2020c); Ghobadpour et al. (2019); Gladek et al. (2017); Herrero et al. (2020); Huang et al. (2017); IEA Bioenergy (2018); IPIFF (2020); Kalantari et al. (2018); Kim et al. (2017); Kumar et al. (2018); Lepage et al. (2021); Melgar-Lalanne et al. (2019); REN21 Renewable Now (2020); Said et al. (2020a); Seyran and Craig (2018); Sridhar et al. (2021); Tomaszewska et al. (2021); Weselek et al. (2019); World Economic Forum, McKinsey & Company (2019); Xie et al. (2020)

In the following paragraphs, each trend is analyzed more in detail.

## 1.4.2 *Renewable Energy in Agriculture*

The agrifood industry has a dual relationship with energy. On the one hand, like any other industry, it requires energy inputs for activities, both in the form of direct energy for land preparation, cultivation, irrigation, harvesting, post-harvest processing, food production, storage, and logistics, and in the form of indirect energy sequestered in fertilizers, herbicides, pesticides, and insecticides (FAO, 2000). On the other hand, agriculture produces raw materials, mainly in the form of biomass, for energy production. In this chapter, the renewable energy in agriculture trend covers a selection of applications related to both the energy use and the production of agricultural biomass for energy generation. More specifically, included here is bioenergy production, intelligent agrivoltaic systems, and solar desalination for irrigation, which have been identified as promising applications of renewable energy in the industry.

### Bioenergy Production

Bioenergy production, which in 2021 accounted for about one-tenth of the world's total primary energy supply (IEA, 2022), includes heat, electricity, gas, and biofuels derived from biomass. Agriculture-derived biomass corresponds to the biodegradable fraction of products, waste and residues of biological origin, including vegetal and animal substances, forestry, and related industries such as fisheries and aquaculture. Biofuels are currently of particular interest as demand is expected to grow by 28% over the next five years (IEA, 2022).

The market potential of biofuels is mainly related to (i) their role as a bridge solution in moving toward a more stringent decarbonization scenario, and (ii) fields of application that cannot be addressed by batteries and hydrogen, which in turn represent the less impacting alternative technologies. For example, biofuels are increasingly being promoted in the aviation industry, where alternative propellants are currently not feasible. On the other hand, biomass combustion and gas derived from biomass would take on a key role as negative-emissions technologies if combined with carbon capture and storage.

Indeed, recent reports by IEA, IPCC, and IRENA consider bioenergy combined with stable geological storage of carbon as an essential option for removing carbon dioxide from the atmosphere. As such, bioenergy is expected to account for up to 20% of the world's energy supply by 2050 (IEA Bioenergy, 2021). Nonetheless, economically viable businesses based on carbon capture and storage have yet to be developed due to the high cost of these technologies.

### Intelligent Agrivoltaics

Conventional agrivoltaic systems are based on the integration of agro-zoological activities on farmland with photovoltaic power plants to produce agricultural products and electricity simultaneously. Intelligent agrivoltaics are enhanced by the adoption of smart devices aimed at boosting the synergy between photovoltaic panels and the soil, increasing overall system efficiency. Smart devices for agrivoltaics include, for example, AI and IoT, as well as water recovery systems. The most promising technological innovations in agrivoltaics are represented by systems capable of allowing photovoltaic panels and crop production to coexist while enhancing their synergy. Examples are panels equipped with both sun-tracking sensors and programmed to respond to crop-specific needs for coverage, or vertical double-sided panels which maximize energy production throughout the entire day and create shaded areas under the panels for flowering plants or preserving ecological microhabitats.

Although current incentives are encouraging the adoption of agrivoltaics, they do not impose any technological standard about the synergies between land and energy production, fostering the diffusion of less expensive, conventional agrivoltaic systems. However, technological upgrades for boosting synergies will be particularly relevant in the near future, when resilience to climate change will be a key feature in crop- and energy-producing activities.

**Solar Desalination for Irrigation**

Solar desalination consists in adopting solar energy as a source for desalination processes for treating seawater, brackish water, or wastewater to derive water usable for irrigation. Seawater reverse osmosis (RO) is currently the most promising technology in the field of desalination. At the moment, RO is accepted as the desalination technology for agriculture since it produces the best quality water and is less energy-demanding than other desalination techniques, which means lower overall costs. More specifically, RO is a water purification technique using a partially permeable membrane to separate ions and other unwanted molecules and particles from water, be it seawater, brackish water, or wastewater. Thanks to its wide availability, seawater is currently receiving the most attention.

Solar desalination for irrigation responds to urgent challenges. On the one hand, global warming is limiting the amount of available freshwater, on the other, population growth, increased consumption, and economic development are expected to be major drivers of water scarcity in the coming decades. In this scenario, agriculture accounts for 70% of the global water demand, making desalination a vital option for the future of the industry. The desalination technology market is augmenting at an annual rate of 7.1% between 2020 and 2028, mostly driven by investments in the Middle East and the Asia Pacific regions, and RO is expected to remain the leading technology in the next few years (Grand View Research, 2020). However, further innovation is needed, focusing on making the RO process more efficient to cut costs and allow large-scale diffusion and application for irrigation. For example, since RO's energy requirements are still high, emerging initiatives are combining it with solar energy production to cut down on its environmental impact.

### *1.4.3 Chemistry and Biotechnology*

Biotechnology is generally defined as "the application of scientific and engineering principles that use living organisms or substances from these organisms to make or modify products, enhance plants or animals, or develop microorganisms for specific uses that are beneficial to humans" (Said et al., 2020a, 2020b). In agriculture, this term refers to any technology entailing biological or chemical processes adopted at a farm level, encompassing a wide cluster of activities including breeding, genetics, microbiome research, synthetic chemistry, and animal health (Burwood-Taylor, 2017).

Today, there is renewed startup activity in this field striving to propose more sustainable new solutions, and an investment wave in M&As from incumbent companies targeting emerging ones (Burwood-Taylor, 2017). Moreover, due to its centrality to the upcoming agrifood industry's challenges, this trend is expected to intensify. In this chapter, biotechnology includes new breeding techniques (NBTs) for plants, livestock, and fish (Laaninen, 2020).

### New Breeding Techniques for Plants

New plant breeding techniques can play a key role in tackling the limited genetic diversity of plants, which reduces their resistance to pests, their capability to use water and nitrogen efficiently, their tolerance to droughts, and their nutritional content and taste (Lusser et al., 2011). NBTs make specific changes to DNA to modify the plant's traits; these modifications can vary in scale from altering a single nitrogen base to inserting or removing one or more genes. The various methods for achieving these changes in traits include: cutting and modifying the genome during the repair process; genome editing to introduce changes to just a few base pairs; transferring a gene from an identical or closely related species (cisgenesis); adding in a reshuffled set of regulatory instructions from same species (intragenesis); deploying processes that alter gene activity without modifying the DNA itself (epigenetic methods); and grafting an unaltered plant onto a genetically modified rootstock.

### New Breeding Techniques for Livestock

New breeding techniques for livestock aim to produce improved breeds of domesticated animals by enhancing their geno-types through selective mating. The main objectives of animal breeding are improved growth rate; increased production and quality of milk, meat, eggs, wool, etc.; better resistance to various diseases; longer productive life; and faster reproduction rate. The more advanced techniques to achieve these objectives include: genomic selection (also called genotyping), the process of determining the DNA sequence at specific positions within the genome of an individual animal, which can be used to determine genes relevant to specific traits or disease; artificial insemination or multiple ovulation embryo transfer technology (MOET); sperm sexing, consisting in the separation of X and Y-sperm for preselecting the desired sex to produce the optimal proportion of males and females in livestock.

### New Breeding Techniques for Fish

New breeding techniques for fish have evolved rapidly in recent years due to these animals' crucial role both for aquaculture and for basic research since they represent the link between invertebrates and vertebrates. Genome editing is currently the most advanced biotechnology for fish, allowing breeders to improve disease resistance and stress tolerance, to enhance rapid growth or sterility traits, and to carry out research on sex determination, growth, development, and immunity. Even though genome editing has rapidly matured in the last decade, some technical obstacles still hinder its widespread application by businesses (the major challenge being the limited success rate of micro-injection). However, recent interest in genome editing for fish is evident from the investments being made by startups and incumbent companies in different countries such as Norway, the USA, Brazil, and Japan, to fuel technological advances and exploit the potential for both theoretical research and commercial purposes (Lu et al., 2021).

### *1.4.4 Novel Farming Systems*

Novel farming systems are new methods of farming living ingredients, many of which are traditionally grown outdoors (Burwood-Taylor & Cosgrove, 2017). The innovators and startups that adopt these systems consider them sustainable as they use fewer natural resources to produce the same quantity of food (or more) per square meter compared to traditional farming systems. Since they could change the paradigm of traditional agriculture, novel farming systems have also emerged as an attractive solution for investors and governments who are looking for solutions to the food security challenge.

In this chapter, the novel farming systems trend encompasses three applications: vertical farming, insect farming, and algae farming.

#### Vertical Farming

Vertical farming is part of the broader indoor farming category and is the practice of cultivating crops indoors in vertically stacked layers, in a controlled environment using soilless farming techniques such as hydroponics, aquaponics, and aeroponics[6] to optimize plant growth conditions. While the innovativeness of vertical farming may be clear from a technological standpoint, the advantages and implications of this new way of farming are not trivial from the investors' standpoint (Financial Times, 2022b). Listed below are the potential environmental and social benefits related to vertical farming (Despommier, 2010).

- Continuous production: The technology behind vertical farming allows year-round production even in non-tropical areas, with much higher productivity than conventional agriculture. The yield of one acre (equal to about 0.40 hectares) cultivated with indoor farming methods is equivalent to the yield of 30 acres (equal to just over 12 hectares) cultivated with traditional methods.

[6]Hydroponics, aeroponics, and aquaponics are agriculture systems that replace soil with nutrient-rich water for plant feeding. Hydroponic systems use only a medium (e.g., sand, gravel, or peat), water and added nutrients to grow plants. Aeroponic systems replace mediums with air: plants' roots are suspended in dark enclosures and sprayed with nutrient-rich solutions. Aquaponic systems, instead, merge hydroponics and aquaculture, growing plants and fishes in a common integrated environment (AlSrouf, 2017).

- Elimination of herbicides and pesticides: The growing conditions of plants in controlled environments make it possible to limit or totally abandon the use of herbicides and pesticides.
- Protection from weather events: Vertical farming, thanks to its structural characteristics, protects crops from extreme weather events such as drought, hail, and floods.
- Water conservation and recycling: Hydroponic cultivation techniques use about 70% less water than traditional agriculture, and aeroponic systems use even less than that (AlShrouf, 2017a, 2017b).
- Reduction of dependence on fossil fuels: Growing plants indoors eliminates the dependence on machinery used in traditional agriculture and therefore cuts the consumption of fossil fuels.
- Reduction of occupational accidents: Vertical farms can cut down on the number of accidents caused by the use of large agricultural equipment and continuous exposure to chemicals.

Notably, the innovativeness of vertical farming lies in its architecture. Vertical farms rely on several technologies, which need to be combined effectively and efficiently to achieve economic and environmental sustainability. In fact, successful technological combinations are not obvious. Although the overall production process replicates across vertical farms, it is almost impossible to recreate the exact same conditions on two different farms; this means that each one needs to apply a specific architectural solution.

### Insect Farming

Insect farming is the practice of raising and breeding insects as livestock. They are cultivated in captivity, and each step in the process is controlled (e.g., living conditions, diet, food quality). Insects may be farmed to produce commodities, such as silk, honey, lac or insect tea, or as a raw material for food or feed. According to the Food and Agriculture Organization of the United Nations (FAO), "Insects have a high food conversion rate: for example, crickets need six times less feed than cattle, four times less than sheep, and twice less than pigs and broiler chickens to produce the same amount of protein" (FAO, 2020). Moreover, insects can serve as a protein-rich substitute for animal feed (even for aquaculture) as they require very little land or energy to grow and they can be produced quickly all year round, unlike other animal feedstock such as soybeans (Burwood-Taylor & Cosgrove, 2017).

Entomophagy is an ancestral practice, and many insect species have been considered feed and food in several countries worldwide for some time now. However, only in the last decades some species (e.g., mealworms, wax worms, crickets, black soldier flies) have begun to be mass raised in controlled indoor environments. Among the above-mentioned species, flies are the fourth most consumed by humans. They are characterized by a large reproductive capacity, short life cycles, and rapid growth rates, and they can eat an extensive variety of organic material as feed. These features make them highly promising from a business perspective, and several applied research laboratories and companies are already beginning to focus on scaling up production to use them as animal feed, composting, waste mitigation, and other non-food applications.

**Algae Farming**

Algae farming, also known as "algae-culture," refers to growing different species of algae for commercial use (Financial Times, 2022c). This is usually done via open-pond systems, photo-bioreactor systems, or a mix of the two. More in detail, macro-algae, which are multi-celled, are relatively easy and cheap to grow, either in open water or in tanks. Therefore, most economic value is added during the processing and extraction of their beneficial compounds. Instead, micro-algae, which are single-celled, must be grown in a controlled setting. They are commonly sold in food stores as nutritional supplements, but can also be used in biofuel, bioplastics, fertilizers, pharmaceuticals, and cosmetics, as well as in animal and fish feeds (Cosgrove, 2017).

While algae farming has been carried out for decades now, its current success is given by the introduction of innovative technologies that make traditional processes more efficient. In other words, the innovativeness of recent algae farming activities lies in the renewed architecture of its production and transformation processes.

Algae farming flexibility in terms of potential applications (e.g., food, feed, pharmaceuticals, energy, plastic materials) makes it appealing from a business perspective. Among others, algae farming for biofuel production is currently one of the main areas of interest. Given the spiking prices in fossil fuels and bans on other vegetable oils, algae-derived oil may gain momentum, with the chance of competing with fossil propellants and electric cars. In fact, the latter still have negative externalities along their supply chains and limited autonomy. So far, looking at its market potential, algae farming represents an underexploited sector within novel farming systems, but it has been estimated that it will reach $45 billion by 2023 (Cosgrove, 2017).

### *1.4.5 Innovative Aquaculture*

While the entire fishing and aquaculture industry has mushroomed in the past decades, responding to a 122% upsurge in demand for fish at a global level from 1990 to 2018, most of this increase has been driven by aquaculture, with an explosion of 527% in global production from 1990 to 2018, reaching a total farm-gate sale value[7] in 2018 of $263.6 billion (FAO, 2022). Aquaculture is the breeding, rearing, and harvesting of fish, shellfish, and other organisms in water environments,

[7]The price of the product available at the farm, excluding the transport and delivery price.

be they located in manmade tanks on land, in the ocean, or in estuaries or ponds. Given its potential to respond to soaring food demand, aquaculture is a lively field for innovation nowadays. For example, one expanding area is the application of a set of sensors to aquaculture production processes and principles of control engineering; the aim here is monitoring, measuring, analyzing, interpreting the space/temporal variability of productions. This provides decision support to farmers to achieve what is known as "precision aquaculture."

However, today recirculating aquaculture systems (RAS) represent the most promising technology in the sector. These closed, controlled systems constantly recirculate and filter water, providing benefits in terms of environmental sustainability and logistics, seeing as they may be placed on land as well. Although RAS have been available for many years, they have recently gained attention in response to raised industrial environmental sustainability standards. Indeed, RAS can respond to many challenges related to traditional aquaculture techniques, such as avoiding the introduction of non-indigenous species outside their range or guaranteeing high water quality with beneficial effects on fish health. Moreover, this technology is of particular interest in highly populated areas, where its applicability on land makes it possible to locate production near suppliers and/or to the final market, cutting transportation costs and environmental impacts.

Although RAS energy requirements are still higher than those of traditional farming systems, consisting of net enclosures located in freshwater, brackish water, and saltwater, these systems are the only technology in the sector that is attracting sizeable investments in aquaculture. These funds are coming from other industries and many countries, from the USA and Norway to Japan and China, and to some extent, also in Southern Europe. As a result, several start-ups that focus on this technology have opened for business and the ongoing R&D activity is expected to reduce RAS energy requirements and costs.

### *1.4.6 Agritech*

Mechanization of farm operations, which includes agricultural tools, equipment and machinery for land preparation, crop management, harvest and post-harvest activities, is a key driver of efficient farming systems and is currently considered an innovation trend in the agribusiness industry. Yet, mechanization is a well-established trend and not a novelty. From the Industrial Revolution onward, agricultural mechanization evolved from basic hand tools and animal-powered implements to sophisticated engine-powered equipment, leading the transition from subsistence-based to market-oriented agriculture (Santos Valle, 2020).

In particular, today the term "Agriculture 4.0" or "Agritech" is used to describe a specific type of agriculture that integrates a series of innovations emerging over the last 15 years or so that serve to enhance crop yields and reduced risks. The result is an optimized design of agricultural machinery by combining equipment with digital data management; nowadays, several technologies are also incorporated such as AI for pest and disease diagnostics, remote sensing (satellite and drone imagery), ground sensors (soil, crop or meteorological stations), and automated equipment for farm operations. All these technologies support the farmer in the operational management of the company (Saiz-Rubio & Rovira-MÃs, 2020). For example, autonomous agricultural robots are replacing manned vehicles in fieldwork. In addition, satellites, drones, and other sensing platforms capture different agronomical parameters and inform farmers about the conditions of soil and groundwater, risks connected to pests and diseases, climate forecasts, or for livestock, animals' health and vital functions. To do so, all the information collected through sensors is processed by specific software through machine learning to support farmers' decision-making.

Today, agritech is already in place and a continuous evolution toward total automation of farm processes is underway. If we look at this trend, there is no single most promising technology so much as the ability to integrate different technologies and combine all the information that they collect: this function is called "interoperability."

## *1.4.7 Alternative Proteins*

> Cars replaced horses, petroleum replaced whales, tractors replaced oxen, telecommunications replaced carrier pigeons, fermentation replaced cows and pigs for insulin production. [...] Wherever we look, humans have consistently built technologies that surpass their animal predecessors. Food may be next.
>
> — Rob Leclerc, founding partner of AgFunder, in 2019

Today we can say that alternatives to animal proteins are already a reality. Applying the latest technologies from biotech, tissue engineering, AI, and food science, inventors and entrepreneurs worldwide are trying (and apparently with success) to create novel foods that are animal-free and, to some extent, possibly more affordable, healthier, and sustainable than traditional food.

"Alternative protein" is a term that encompasses a series of protein-rich ingredients sourced from plants, insects, fungi, or through tissue culture; the aim is to replace conventional animal-based sources. In this chapter, the alternative protein trend includes three applications, namely cultivated meat, fermentation-derived products, and plant-based meat. Notably, proteins derived from insects are analyzed separately in Sect. 1.4.4 since insect farming and related activities have been assimilated to livestock.

### Cultivated Meat

Cultivated meat (or cultured meat), which actually includes seafood as well, is produced by cultivating animal cells directly. It is made of the same cell types arranged in the same or similar structure as animal tissues, thus replicating the sensory and nutritional profiles of conventional meat. This production method eliminates the need to raise farm animals. The manufacturing process of cultivated meat begins with acquiring and banking stem cells from an animal. These cells are then grown in bioreactors (or cultivators) at high densities and volumes. Similar to what happens inside an animal's body, cells are fed by an oxygen-rich cell-culture medium made of basic nutrients such as amino acids, glucose, vitamins, and inorganic salts, and supplemented with proteins and other growth factors. Changes in the medium composition trigger immature cells to differentiate into the skeletal muscle, fat, and connective tissues that constitute meat. The differentiated cells are then harvested, prepared, and packaged into final products.

Although animal cell culture in food is applied primarily to cultivated meat production, a similar process can be used to produce milk, eggs, gelatin, and other foodstuffs. However, the technologies applied in these cases are not broadly validated, there are only a few commercial players on the market; not all are able to present investors with a solid investment case (Financial Times, 2022d). For this reason, cultivated meat is the most cited application and currently represents the most promising subsector in the field.

### Fermentation-Derived Proteins

Fermentation-derived proteins can be either final products (e.g., ground meat, whole-cut meats, dairy, eggs, and pet food) or ingredients (e.g., fats and oils, growth factors) and can be produced in three different ways:

1. Traditional fermentation, which uses intact live microorganisms to modulate and process plant-derived ingredients, resulting in products with unique flavor and nutritional profiles and modified texture.
2. Biomass fermentation, which leverages the fast growth and high protein content of many microorganisms to produce large quantities of proteins.
3. Precision fermentation, which uses specifically designed microbial hosts as "cell factories" to produce specific functional ingredients. These ingredients are powerful enablers of improved sensory characteristics and functional attributes of plant-based products or cultivated meat.

Although all three methods used to produce proteins derived from fermentation are used today, the most innovative and at the same time fastest growing technology is precision fermentation. In 2020, 13 startups dedicated to the use of fermentation for alternative proteins were launched; nine were based on precision fermentation.

### Plant-Based Meat

Plant-based meat is a term used to refer to food products made from vegetarian or vegan ingredients and eaten as a replacement for meat. Meat alternatives typically approximate qualities of specific types of meat, such as mouthfeel, flavor, appearance, or chemical characteristics. Likewise, plant-based dairy and eggs are alternatives to animal-derived food such as milk, cheese, yogurt, and eggs. Alternatives to meat like tofu date back a thousand years, and several companies currently leading the plant-based meat market opened from the 1970s to the 1990s. But only recently the market has extended beyond the vegetarian and vegan consumer niche, mostly because producers have honed their ability to mimic meat features, and plant-based products have a smaller environmental footprint.

Today, inflation triggered by the Ukraine war is squeezing consumer income and inflating food prices, severely limiting people's willingness to pay higher prices for plant-based products (among many others) and slowing the growth in sales registered in the last few years. However, at a world level, there are more than 780 companies whose core focus is on plant-based meat, seafood, egg, or dairy, and all the biggest animal agriculture firms are investing in these food items (Financial Times, 2022e; Foreign Policy Magazine, 2022; Good Food Institute, 2021).

### *1.4.8 Food Safety and Traceability*

According to the World Health Organization, food safety is closely related to nutrition and food security, as unsafe food is a major cause of disease and malnutrition, affecting children, the elderly, and the sick in particular today. Moreover, a lack of food safety is preventing socioeconomic development, stressing healthcare systems, national economies, and trade (WHO, 2015). However, global concern over food safety is pushing innovation in the agrifood sector. In this chapter, the food safety and traceability trend encompasses food preservation and food traceability technologies as well as smart packaging.

**Food Preservation Technologies**

Food preservation technologies aim to treat and handle food to extend shelf life and prevent foodborne illness while preserving nutritional value, color, texture, and flavor. Food preservation techniques can be traced back to our ancestors, who found ways to store food and keep it edible by sun drying, salting, and pasteurization; in the more recent industrialization period, thermal treatments, canning, and freezing were introduced. New techniques call for continuous research, and the full technological development and market potential in this area are far from being reached.

Promising food preservation technologies vary depending on the item in question, its spoilage mechanism, and the relative supply chain stage. In this complex equation, several promising technologies can be found and applied. Advances in *thermal treatment* have brought about significant progress in the food industry, including treatments that combine electrical methods with the well-proven technique of heating food (e.g., electroplasmolysis, ohmic heating, and microwave heating) and advanced freezing techniques (e.g., high-pressure freezing, ultrasound-assisted freezing, electromagnetic disturbance freezing, and dehydration freezing). *Ultrasound treatments*, subjecting food products to high-intensity, high-frequency sound waves, are particularly promising thanks to the simplicity of the equipment and the reduced costs with respect to other preservation solutions. *Ozone treatment* (in some cases combined with ultrasound) is also gaining relevance in response to consumer interest in additive-free food since ozone quickly decomposes. *Pulsed electric field treatments* are more and more in demand in every food sector due to the short duration of the high-intensity electric field, and the capability of enhancing nutritive qualities, safety, and shelf life. *Natural preservatives* are safe and present great antioxidant and antimicrobial properties. These may eventually substitute processed food and are also a vibrant field of research. Finally, *nanotechnologies* represent a major step forward as they can provide slow-release action, address specific targets with precision, do not release pollutants, and are energy and space efficient. These include any material or nanoparticle with one or more dimensions to the order of 100 nm or less. Nanotechnologies can be applied in agriculture activities (e.g., nanosensors for precision agriculture, nanomaterials for agrochemicals), food processing (e.g., sensorial attributes to enhance flavor or nutrient delivery to plants), and food packaging.

### Smart Packaging: Active, Intelligent, and Connected

Smart packaging technologies include intelligent, connected, active packaging. They use sensors to collect sourcing, safety, and traceability information regarding the production, processing, environmental footprint, quality, and safety of food. Then they share this information with users (intelligent), communicate with other packages, smart appliances, or the internet (connected), and intervene on the food or the environment surrounding it, adding or removing components, to increase shelf life (active). Currently, to upgrade the effectiveness of smart packaging, the most promising technologies are sensors for collecting and transmitting information and natural material capable of releasing shelf-life-extending substances.

In 2020, the size of the smart packaging global market was $22 million and is expected to reach more than $38 million by 2030, with a compound annual growth rate (CAGR) of 5.5% from 2021 to 2030. Intelligent packaging, in particular, is expected to show a higher CAGR in the same decade (Allied Market Research, 2022). At the same time, another high-potential technology is biodegradable materials, whose commercialization is projected to grow in the next few years. Made of materials that can be rapidly decomposed into natural elements by microorganisms, biodegradable packaging responds to the escalating need to reduce the environmental burden of packaging solutions.

### Smart Traceability

This generally refers to traceability enabled by technological solutions and aimed at improving food safety using advanced detection technologies and digital technologies for analyzing traceability data. The core principles of smart food traceability are: (i) leveraging portable sensors and indicators to more comprehensive, traceable, and timely data about food products, and (ii) developing novel traceability technologies by incorporating emerging digital technologies, such as the IoT and cloud computing. Nowadays, there are several technologies used to trace food along the supply chain:

- digital technologies such as IoT and real-time tracking and monitoring, blockchain solutions, and AI- and ML-based data analytics,
- electronic technologies such as Radio-Frequency Identification (RFID) and smart sensors,
- electromagnetic imaging such as X-ray inspection and hyperspectral imaging,
- chemical and biomolecule fingerprinting, including rapid molecular and chemical diagnostics for food pathogen testing.

Food traceability has the potential to improve public health by monitoring food safety, and to make the supply chain more resilient, to curb food waste, and to monitor the industry's environmental and social impacts (Unnikrishnan et al., 2021), supporting the response to several of the agrifood's major challenges. This trend now seems to be gaining momentum. In particular, after several years of effort to trace food from source to final consumers, more and more countries are now adopting laws that hold food producers accountable for the activities they carry out along their entire supply chain.

### *1.4.9 E-commerce*

**Food Delivery Ecosystems**

Food delivery is a form of e-commerce and an online-to-offline business in which consumers place orders for food or grocery items online and receive the goods at an offline outlet. This trend, together with the spread of e-commerce in all businesses, has been driven mainly by the following factors: increased disposable income (particularly in developing nations), upgraded broadband penetration and smartphone proliferation, improved reliability of electronic payments, and expanded delivery networks.

Food delivery providers can be categorized as either restaurant-to-consumer delivery or platform-to-consumer delivery operators. The former make the food and deliver it. As for the latter, when the order to a restaurant is made via a third-party platform, they can provide online delivery services from partner restaurants that do not necessarily offer delivery services themselves (Li et al., 2020).

While initially food delivery operators acted mainly as restaurant aggregators, simply taking orders from customers and directing them to restaurants, which handle the delivery themselves, in the last decade new delivery players have come on the scene. More in detail, these newcomers rely on their own logistics network, providing delivery for restaurants that do not have their own drivers or acting as supermarket competitors in delivering food directly to the home. In the latter case, we refer to companies that base their competitiveness on the proximity of retail space to consumers' homes, which they reach through a widespread network of "dark stores" (i.e., large retail facilities that resemble conventional supermarkets or other stores but are not open to the public, housing goods used to fulfill orders placed online).

These stores make it possible to rapidly fill consumers' orders while reducing several expenditures. In fact, the front office is relegated to the online platform, and the store performs the function of a warehouse; consequently, space is optimized for picking, preparing, and fulfilling delivery orders. This proximity to consumers' homes also diminishes "last-mile" delivery cost, which is considered to be the most expensive portion of supply chain logistics (Altenried, 2019).

Notably, the Covid-19 pandemic played a crucial role in this businesses' development (McKinsey, 2021): social distancing requirements and stay-at-home orders favored the development of e-commerce and in particular of food delivery.

## 1.5 Conclusion

This chapter has described how the world's industries and economies are affected by several forces of change. Among these, some seem to be more pervasive and impactful, even going so far as to influence other phenomena of the same scale, enhancing or diverting their effects. Interacting with sector peculiarities, megatrends and driving forces assume industry-specific forms and relevance. In the case of the agribusiness sector, while megatrends impel it to transform its traditional dynamics and production models, as is the case in many other industries, its centrality for the prosperity of human societies turns megatrends into challenges that must be faced in the coming years—namely, boosting agricultural productivity, handling food loss and waste, using natural resources efficiently and enhancing ecosystem services, improving public nutrition and health, and better distributing value along the supply chain. To tackle most of these challenges, technological innovations will prove to be crucial. Indeed, many promising innovations are emerging all along the agribusiness value chain. However, given the latter's complexity, its tight links with other evolving sectors, and the disparate technical and economic development levels of technological innovations, to fully understand the possible evolutions of this complex scenario we need a more in-depth analysis. The next chapter will delve into technological innovations, investigating their typology (i.e., product, process, or business model innovation), technical and business readiness, the scopes that they serve, and the value chain actors that would potentially be interested.

# References

## *Megatrends Analysis: Literary Sources*


BlackRock. (2018). *Megatrends: A research study looking at structural shifts in the global economy and how they affect our investment thinking.*

Boumphrey, S., & Brehmer, Z. (2018). *Megatrend analysis: Putting the consumer at the heart of business.* Euromonitor International.

Deloitte. (2017). *Beyond the noise: The megatrends of tomorrow's world.*

European Environmental Agency. (2018). *Global megatrends and planetary boundaries.*

European Parliament. (2017). *Global trends to 2035. Geo-politics and international power.*

European Strategy and Policy Analysis System. (2015). *Global trends to 2030: Can the EU meet the challenges ahead?* Publications Office of the European Union.

European Union Commission. (2018). *Competence Centre on Foresight – Megatrends Hub.*

EYQ. (2018). *What's after what's next? The upside of disruption: Megatrends shaping 2018 and beyond.*

FAO. (2017a). *The future of food and agriculture: Trends and challenges.*

Fornasiero, R., Sardesai, S., Barros, A. C., & Matopoulos, A. (2021). *Next generation supply chains: A roadmap for research and innovation* (p. 290). Springer Nature.

Forum for the Future. (2019). *Driving systems change in turbulent times: The future of sustainability 2019.*

IPSOS. (2020). *Global trends 2020.*

Laudicina, P., Peterson, E., & Rickert McCaffrey, C. (2018). *Competition, disruption, and deception: Global trends 2018–2023.* A.T. Kearney Global Business Policy Council.

McKinsey & Company. (2017). *McKinsey special collections: Trends and global force*s. Selected Articles from the Strategy and Corporate Finance Practice.

OECD. (2016). *OECD science, technology and innovation outlook 2016.*

Office of the Director of National Intelligence. (2021). *Global trends 2040. A more contested world.*

Pano, L. A. (2019). *The changing faces of aid: 4 Trends that may be widening inequality.* BOND.

PWC. (2019). *Megatrends.*

Retief, F., Bond, A., Pope, J., Morrison-Saunders, A., & King, N. (2016). Global megatrends and their implications for environmental assessment practice. *Environmental Impact Assessment Review, 61*, 52–60.

Sardá, R., & Pogutz, S. (2018). *Corporate sustainability in the 21st century: Increasing the resilience of social-ecological systems.* Routledge.

Sydney Business Insights. (2019). *Megatrends.*

Trend One. (2019). *Megatrends.*

UNDESA – United Nations, Department of Economic and Social Affairs. (2019). *Sustainable Development Outlook 2019: Gathering storms and silver linings.*

UNDP and UNRISD. (2017). *Global trends: Challenges and opportunities in the implementation of the sustainable development goals.*

Wall, S. (2018). *Megatrends: Predicting the future to reinvent today.* HP.

Winston, A. R. (2019). *The world in 2030: Nine megatrends to watch.* Massachusetts Institute of Technology Sloan Management Review.

Z_punkt. (2019). *Megatrends.*

## Agribusiness Megatrends and Challenges Analysis Literary Sources

FAO. (2017b). *The future of food and agriculture – Trends and challenges*. Rome.

FAO. (2018). *The future of food and agriculture – Alternative pathways to 2050*. Rome.

Kirova, M., Montanari, F., Ferreira, I., Pesce, M., Albuquerque, J. D., Montfort, C., Neirynck, R., Moroni, J., Traon, D., Perrin, M., Echarri, J., Arcos Pujades, A., Lopez Montesinos, E., & Pelayo, E. (2019). *Research for AGRI Committee – Megatrends in the agrifood sector*, European Parliament, Policy Department for Structural and Cohesion Policies, Brussels.

Maggio, A., Scapolo, F., van Criekinge, T., & Serraj, R. (2019). Global drivers and megatrends in agrifood systems. In *Agriculture & Food Systems to 2050: Global Trends, Challenges and Opportunities*. European Parliament. Brussels.

OECD/FAO. (2021). *OECD-FAO Agricultural Outlook 2021–2030*. OECD Publishing.

## Technological Innovations Analysis Literary Sources

Ag Funder. (2020). *2020 Farm Tech, Investing Report*.

Agrilyst. (2016). *State of indoor farming*.

Ahmad, N., Alharthi, F., Alam, M., Wahab, R., Manoharadas, S., & Alrayes, B. (2021). Syngas production via $CO_2$ reforming of methane over $SrNiO_3$ and $CeNiO_3$ perovskites. *Energies, 14*(10), 2928.

AlShrouf, A. (2017a). Hydroponics, aeroponic and aquaponic as compared with conventional farming. *American Scientific Research Journal for Engineering, Technology, and Sciences (ASRJETS), 27*(1), 247–255.

Amit, S. K., Uddin, M. M., Rahman, R., Islam, S. R., & Khan, M. S. (2017). A review on mechanisms and commercial aspects of food preservation and processing. *Agriculture & Food Security, 6*(1), 1–22.

Antonucci, F., & Costa, C. (2020). Precision aquaculture: A short review on engineering innovations. *Aquaculture International, 28*(1), 41–57.

Araújo, R., Vázquez Calderón, F., Sánchez López, J., Azevedo, I. C., Bruhn, A., Fluch, S., et al. (2021). Current status of the algae production industry in Europe: An emerging sector of the Blue Bioeconomy. *Frontiers in Marine Science, 7*, 1247.

Ashok, J., Dewangan, N., Das, S., Hongmanorom, P., Wai, M. H., Tomishige, K., & Kawi, S. (2020). Recent progress in the development of catalysts for steam reforming of biomass tar model reaction. *Fuel Processing Technology, 199*, 106252.

Baiano, A. (2020). Edible insects: An overview on nutritional characteristics, safety, farming, production technologies, regulatory framework, and socio-economic and ethical implications. *Trends in Food Science & Technology, 100*, 35–50.

Bayer Crop Science Division. (2021). *Shaping the future of agriculture*.

Behzadi, G., O'Sullivan, M. J., Olsen, T. L., & Zhang, A. (2018). Agribusiness supply chain risk management: A review of quantitative decision models. *Omega, 79*, 21–42.

Biggs, L., & Giles, D. (2013). *Current and future agricultural practices and technologies which affect fuel efficiency*. Intelligent Energy Europe-European Commission.

Birkby, J. (2016). *Vertical farming*. ATTRA Sustainable Agriculture. National Centre for Appropriate Technology.

Daghari, I., & El Zarroug, M. R. (2020). Concepts review of solar desalination technologies for irrigation. *Journal of New Sciences, 71*, 4319–4326.

De Clercq, M., Vats, A., Biel, A., & in collaboration with Oliver Wyman. (2018). *Agriculture 4.0: The future of farming technology*. World Government Summit.

Dossey, A. T., Morales-Ramos, J. A., & Rojas, M. G. (Eds.). (2016). *Insects as sustainable food ingredients: Production, processing and food applications*. Academic Press.

Drago, E., Campardelli, R., Pettinato, M., & Perego, P. (2020). Innovations in smart packaging concepts for food: An extensive review. *Food, 9*(11), 1628.
Duhan, J. S., Kumar, R., Kumar, N., Kaur, P., Nehra, K., & Duhan, S. (2017). Nanotechnology: The new perspective in precision agriculture. *Biotechnology Reports, 15*, 11–23.
EY. (2020). *The Norwegian aquaculture analysis 2020.*
FAO. (2000). *Environment and Natural Resources Working Paper No. 4.* Rome.
Five Seasons Ventures. (2019). *The State of European Food Tech 2019.*
GFI. (2020a). *State of the industry report: Cultivated Meat.*
GFI. (2020b). *State of the industry report: Fermentation.*
GFI. (2020c). *State of the industry report: Plant-based meat, eggs, and dairy.*
Ghobadpour, A., Boulon, L., Mousazadeh, H., Malvajerdi, A. S., & Rafiee, S. (2019). State of the art of autonomous agricultural off-road vehicles driven by renewable energy systems. *Energy Procedia, 162*, 4–13.
Gladek, E., Fraser, M., Roemers, G., Muñoz, O., Kennedy, E., & Hirsch, P. (2017). The global food system: An analysis. *Meta.*
Herrero, M., Thornton, P. K., Mason-D'Croz, D., et al. (2020). Innovation can accelerate the transition towards a sustainable food system. *Nature Food, 1*, 266–272.
Huang, H. W., Wu, S. J., Lu, J. K., Shyu, Y. T., & Wang, C. Y. (2017). Current status and future trends of high-pressure processing in food industry. *Food Control, 72*, 1–8.
IEA Bioenergy. (2018). *Hydrogen from biomass gasification.*
IPIFF. (2020). *Guide on good hygiene practices for EU producers of insects as food and feed.*
Kalantari, F., Tahir, O. M., Joni, R. A., & Fatemi, E. (2018). Opportunities and challenges in sustainability of vertical farming: A review. *Journal of Landscape Ecology, 11*(1), 35–60.
Kim, J. K., Yarish, C., Hwang, E. K., Park, M., & Kim, Y. (2017). Seaweed aquaculture: Cultivation technologies, challenges and its ecosystem services. *Algae, 32*(1), 1–13.
Kumar, R., Ahmed, M., Bhadrachari, G., & Thomas, J. P. (2018). Desalination for agriculture: Water quality and plant chemistry, technologies and challenges. *Water Science and Technology: Water Supply, 18*(5), 1505–1517.
Lepage, T., Kammoun, M., Schmetz, Q., & Richel, A. (2021). Biomass-to-hydrogen: A review of main routes production, processes evaluation and techno-economical assessment. *Biomass and Bioenergy, 144*, 105920.
Melgar-Lalanne, G., Hernández-Álvarez, A. J., & Salinas-Castro, A. (2019). Edible insects processing: Traditional and innovative technologies. *Comprehensive Reviews in Food Science and Food Safety, 18*(4), 1166–1191.
REN21 Renewable Now. (2020). *Renewables 2020 Global status report.*
Said, S., Agung, P. P., Putra, W. P. B., & Kaiin, E. M. (2020a). The role of biotechnology in animal production. In *IOP conference series: Earth and environmental science* (Vol. 492, No. 1, p. 012035). IOP Publishing.
Seyran, E., & Craig, W. (2018). New breeding techniques and their possible regulation. *AgBioforum, 21*(1), 1–12.
Sridhar, A., Ponnuchamy, M., Kumar, P. S., & Kapoor, A. (2021). Food preservation techniques and nanotechnology for increased shelf life of fruits, vegetables, beverages and spices: A review. *Environmental Chemistry Letters, 19*(2), 1715–1735.
Tomaszewska, B., Akkurt, G. G., Kaczmarczyk, M., Bujakowski, W., Keles, N., Jarma, Y. A., et al. (2021). Utilization of renewable energy sources in desalination of geothermal water for agriculture. *Desalination, 513*, 115151.
Weselek, A., Ehmann, A., Zikeli, S., Lewandowski, I., Schindele, S., & Högy, P. (2019). Agrophotovoltaic systems: Applications, challenges, and opportunities. A review. *Agronomy for Sustainable Development, 39*(4), 1–20.
World Economic Forum, McKinsey & Company. (2019). *Innovation with a purpose: Improving traceability in food value chains through technology innovations.*
Xie, Y., Xu, Z., Wu, Z., & Hong, L. (2020). Sex manipulation technologies progress in livestock: A review. *Frontiers in Veterinary Science, 7.*

## Other References

Aguilar, F. J. (1967, Oct). Scanning the business environment. *The Journal of Business, 40*(4), 537–539.

Allied Market Research. (2022). *Smart packaging market. Report.*

AlShrouf, A. (2017b). Hydroponics, aeroponic and aquaponic as compared with conventional farming. *American Academic Scientific Research Journal for Engineering, Technology, and Sciences, 27*(1), 247–255.

Altenried, M. (2019). On the last mile: Logistical urbanism and the transformation of labour. Workorganisation, labour & globalisation. *Pluto Journals, 13*(1), 114–129.

Aquastat. (2014). *Water withdrawal by sector*. Retrieved from http://www.fao.org/nr/aquastat

Brooks, S. (2005). Biotechnology and the politics of truth: From the green revolution to an evergreen revolution. *Sociologia Ruralis, 45*(4), 360–379.

Burwood-Taylor, L. (2017). *What is agriculture biotechnology?* AgFunderNews. Retrieved from https://agfundernews.com/what-is-agriculture-biotechnology

Burwood-Taylor, L., & Cosgrove, E. (2017). *What are novel farming systems?* AgFunderNews. Retrieved from https://agfundernews.com/what-are-novel-farming-systems

Castelli, G., Meregalli, S., & Pennarola, F. (Eds.). (2022). *The post-digital enterprise: Going beyond the hype*. Springer Nature.

CCRI. (2021). *Resilience – Addressing physical climate risks in infrastructure investment.*

CDRI. (2021). *Infrastructure Standards – Building Blocks for a Resilient Future – Technical Note.*

COPA-COGECA. (2018). *The agri food supply chain and the unfair trading practices*. Bruxelles.

Cosgrove, E. (2017). *Algae Market to Reach $45bn by 2023*. AgFunderNews. Retrieved from https://agfunsdernews.com/report-algae-market-could-to-reach-45b-by-2023

Credit Suisse. (2017). *Supertrends – One year on. The future now – Investing for the long term*, May.

Downey, D. W., & Erickson, S. P. (1987). *Agribusiness management*. McGraw-Hill.

Davis, J. H. (1995). «*Business Responsibility and the Market for Farm Products*», address to Boston conference on distribution, 17 October 1955.

Deconinck, K. (2020). *Concentration in seed and biotech markets: Extent, causes, and impacts*. Organisation for Economic Co-Operation and Development (OECD), Annual Review of Resource Economics.

Despommier, D. (2010). *The vertical farm: feeding the world in the 21st century*. Macmillan.

Dixon, J., Omwega, A. M., Friel, S., Burns, C., Donati, K., & Carlisle, R. (2007). The health equity dimensions of urban food systems. *Journal of Urban Health, 84*, 118–129.

Fałkowski, J., Ménard, C., Sexton, R.J., Swinnen J., & Vandevelde S. (Authors), Di Marcantonio, F., and Ciaian, P. (Editors) (2017). *Unfair trading practices in the food supply chain: A literature review on methodologies, impacts and regulatory aspects*. European Commission, Joint Research Centre.

FAO. (2015). *FAOSTAT*. Retrieved from http://faostat3.fao.org/home/E.

FAO. (2020). Retrieved from https://www.fao.org/edible-insects/en/.

FAO. (2021). *Supply chain joins deforestation and farming practices as main source of emissions in agrifood sector*. Retrieved from https://www.fao.org/newsroom/detail/supply-chain-is-growing-source-of-agrifood-GHG-emissions/en.

FAO. (2022). *The state of world fisheries and aquaculture 2022*. Towards Blue Transformation. Rome, FAO. https://doi.org/10.4060/cc0461en

FAO, IFAD, UNICEF, WFP and WHO. (2022). The state of food security and nutrition in the world 2022. *Repurposing food and agricultural policies to make healthy diets more affordable*. Rome, FAO. https://doi.org/10.4060/cc0639en.

Financial Times Lex Comment. (2022a). *Life expectancy: Drop in US longevity is rooted in poverty*. Available at: https://www.ft.com/content/b39480b4-00f3-4112-b24c-bfae825e4a2b

Financial Times. (2022b). *The big read – America's new agricultural frontier: vertical farms*. July 12. Available at: https://www.ft.com/content/4263fbe2-db0e-4a8e-8cb4-32405ee2c9b6
Financial Times. (2022c). *Lex Comment – Algae start-ups: From pond slime to dinner time*. 9 October. Available at: https://www.ft.com/content/5205ef80-7140-4431-a5fe-41bf9ed20016
Financial Times. (2022d). *Lab-grown meat maker Eat Just unable to capitalise on Malaysia chicken ban*, 28 June. Available at: https://www.ft.com/content/f986f084-9bb7-4f3a-a91b-1a5c783fc257.
Financial Times. (2022e). *Inflation kills off hopes for return of plant-based meat boom*. 19 September. Available at: https://www.ft.com/content/9cb81801-eb42-455c-ad3e-805fb9bd46c7
Foley, J., Ramankutty, N., Brauman, K., et al. (2011). Solutions for a cultivated planet. *Nature, 478*, 337–342.
Foreign Policy Magazine. (2022). *Plant-Based Proteins Are Too Expensive*. 8 October. Available at: https://foreignpolicy.com/2022/10/08/alternative-protein-meat-agriculture-food-security-plant-based-environment/?ct=t(EMAIL_CAMPAIGN_10_13_2022_22_48)&goal=0_8e101ace96-faae95d72a-99765197&mc_cid=faae95d72a&mc_eid=f7f54d653f
Gatti, S., & Chiarella, C. (2020). The future of infrastructure investing – Challenges and opportunities for investors and asset managers. In S. Gatti & C. Chiarella (Eds.), *Disruption in the infrastructure sector*. Springer.
Global Panel on Agriculture and Food Systems for Nutrition. (2016). *Food systems and diets: Facing the challenges of the 21st century*. London, UK, p. 133.
Gorton, M., Lemke, F., & Alfarsi, F. (2017). *Methodological framework: Review of approaches applied in the literature to analyse the occurrence and impact of UTPs*. Paper presented at the workshop on 'Unfair Trading Practices in the Food Supply Chain', European Commission, Brussels 17–18 July 2017.
Good Food Institute. (2021). *2021 State of the Industry Report: Plant-based meat, seafood, eggs, and dairy*.
Goodman, D., & Redclift, M. (1991). *Refashioning nature: Food, ecology and culture*. Routledge.
Grand View Research. (2020). *Water desalination equipment market size, share & trends*.
Griffin, K. (1979). *The political economy of agrarian change: An essay on the green revolution*. Macmillan Press.
Haddad, L., Hawkes, C., Webb, P., et al. (2016). A new global research agenda for food. *Nature, 540*, 30–32.
Hajkowicz, S. (2015). *Global megatrends: Seven patterns of change shaping our future*. CSIRO Publishing.
Hofrichter, S. (2017). *The economics of populism: Why populism matters to growth and markets*, Update – Allianz Global Investors, Number 3, October.
IEA Bioenergy. (2021). *Annual report 2021*. Pearse Buckley, IEA Bioenergy Secretary, Dublin, Ireland.
IEA Bioenergy. (2022). *Bioenergy*. Retrieved from: https://www.iea.org/fuels-and-technologies/bioenergy.
IFAD – Fund for Agricultural Development. (2016). Agrifood markets and value chains. *In Rural Development Report, 2016*, 225–247.
Intergovernmental Panel on Climate Change (IPCC). (2014). *Fifth assessment report – Mitigation of climate change*. Retrieved from http://www.ipcc.ch/report/ar5/wg3/
KPMG International. (2013). *The agricultural and food value chain: Entering a new era of cooperation*.
Laaninen, T. (2020). *New plant-breeding techniques*. EPRS | European Parliamentary Research Service. Members' Research Service, PE 659.343.
Li, C., Mirosa, M., & Bremer, P. (2020). Review of online food delivery platforms and their impacts on sustainability. *Sustainability, 12*(14), 5528.
Lu, J., Fang, W., Huang, J., & Li, S. (2021). The application of genome editing technology in fish. *Marine Life Science & Technology, 3*(3), 326–346.

Lusser, M., Parisi, C., Plan, D., & Rodríguez-Cerezo, E. (2011). *New plant breeding techniques: State-of-the-art and prospects for commercial development (JRC Report EUR 24760 EN)*. Seville, Spain: European Commission Joint Research Centre (JRC).

Matthey, H. (2021). *Trends in global agriculture*. UNCTAD Multiyear Expert Meeting on Commodities and Development, 12thSession.

McKinsey. (2021). *Ordering in: The rapid evolution of food delivery*.

Naisbitt, J., & Aburdene, P. (1990). *Megatrends 2000: 10 New Directions for the 1990s*. New York, Morrow.

OECD. (2022). *Meat consumption indicator*. Retrieved from: https://data.oecd.org/agroutput/meat-consumption.htm

Oxfam. (2018). *Ripe the change*. Oxfam GB, Oxfam House, John Smith Drive, Cowley, Oxford, OX4 2JY, UK.

Pęciak, R. (2016). Megatrends and their implications in the globalised world. *Horyzonty Polityki, 7*(21), 167–184.

Pingali, & Prabhu, L. (2006). *Agricultural growth and economic development: A view through the globalization lens*. 2006 Annual Meeting, August 12–18, 2006, Queensland, Australia 25429, International Association of Agricultural Economists.

Ritchie, H. (2017). *How much of the world's land would we need in order to feed the global population with the average diet of a given country?* Published online at OurWorldInData.org. Available at: https://ourworldindata.org/agricultural-land-by-global-diets

Ritchie, H., & Roser, M. (2013). *Land use*. Published online at OurWorldInData.org

Said, S., et al. (2020b). *The role of biotechnology in animal production*. IOP Conf. Ser.: Earth Environ. Sci. 492 012035.

Saiz-Rubio, V., & Rovira-Más, F. (2020). From smart farming towards agriculture 5.0: A review on crop data management. *Agronomy, 10*(2), 207.

Santos Valle, S. (2020). *Agriculture 4.0 – Agricultural robotics and automated equipment for sustainable crop production*, FAO. Retrieved from https://policycommons.net/artifacts/1422028/agriculture-40/2036099/.

Sexton, R. (2017). *The unfair trading practices in the food supply chain: Types of UTPs*. Paper presented at the workshop on 'Unfair Trading Practices in the Food Supply Chain', European Commission, Brussels, 17–18 July 2017.

Societe Generale Cross Asset Research. (2019). *Water at a crossroads – Today's scarcity, tomorrow's crisis*, February.

The World Counts. (2022). *Meat consumption*. Retrieved from: https://www.theworldcounts.com/challenges/foods-and-beverages/world-consumption-of-meat

UNDESA – United Nations, Department of Economic and Social Affairs, Population Division. (2019a). *World population prospects 2019: Highlights (ST/ESA/SER.A/423)*. New York: United Nations.

UNDESA – United Nations, Department of Economic and Social Affairs, Population Division. (2019b). *World urbanization prospects: The 2018 revision (ST/ESA/SER.A/420)*. New York: United Nations.

UNDESA – United Nations, Department of Economic and Social Affairs. (2017). *The world population prospects: The 2017 revision*.

Unnikrishnan, S., von Koeller, E., Mutz, M., Fovargue, H., & Yong, K., (2021). *The time is ripe for food traceability*. Boston Consulting Group. on 03 May 2022.

Vandermerwe, S., & Rada, J. (1988). Servitization of business: Adding value by adding services. *European Management Journal, 6*(4), 314–324.

West, P. C., Gerber, J. S., Engstrom, P. M., Mueller, N. D., Brauman, K. A., Carlson, K. M., et al. (2014). Leverage points for improving global food security and the environment. *Science, 345*(6194), 325–328.

WHO. (2021). *Obesity and overweight.* Retrieved from: https://www.who.int/news-room/fact-sheets/detail/obesity-and-overweight

WHO. (2015). *WHO estimates of the global burden of foodborne diseases: Foodborne disease burden epidemiology reference group 2007–2015.* World Health Organization https://apps.who.int/iris/handle/10665/199350.

WWF. (2022). *Food loss and waste.* Retrieved from: https://wwf.panda.org/discover/our_focus/food_practice/food_loss_and_waste/

# Chapter 2
# Innovation Trends in the Agribusiness Supply Chain

**Vitaliano Fiorillo, Marianna Lo Zoppo, and Aristea Saputo**

## 2.1 Introduction

The term innovation literally refers to every novelty, change, or transformation that radically modifies or causes an effective renewal in a political or social order, a production method, or a technique. As for innovation in companies, this can take different forms and manifest in different phases of the company's life cycle. According to Schumpeter (1934, p.76), from the perspective of creating new combinations, innovation should cover five areas: (a) the introduction of a new product or service; (b) the introduction of a new method or production process; (c) the creation of a new market; (d) the acquisition of a new source of raw materials or semi-manufactured goods; (e) the establishment of a new organization in any industry, creating a new business or a new market structure leveraging on a certain unique feature of the firm.

In this chapter, we focus on technological innovation, i.e., based on the industrial application of scientific and/or technological knowledge (Cantú & Zapata, 2006). "Innovation" and "technology" are two concepts that are strongly linked and sometimes used interchangeably (Rogers, 2003). However, we distinguish innovation from *technological* innovation, as the former is a broader concept that can encompass various aspects: organizational, social, economic, technological, and strategic (Freeman, 1982; Cantú & Zapata, 2006; Hernandez, 2009).

The advancement of scientific and technological knowledge, and the industrial application of this new knowledge, are the keys to the agribusiness industry's future development for at least two reasons. First, for companies, to innovate means to remain competitive. Innovation also has the power to make the demand curve less

V. Fiorillo (✉) · M. Lo Zoppo · A. Saputo
AGRI Lab, SDA Bocconi School of Management, Milan, Italy
e-mail: vitaliano.fiorillo@sdabocconi.it; marianna.lozoppo@sdabocconi.it; aristea.saputo@sdabocconi.it



S. Gatti et al. (eds.), *Agriculture as an Alternative Investment*, Contributions to Finance and Accounting, https://doi.org/10.1007/978-3-031-27918-8_2

elastic to price: when customers find that the proposed solution to their needs is extremely effective, they translate this benefit into lower price sensitivity. Clearly, this only happens when the innovation in question makes all previous solutions outdated and ineffective. Furthermore, innovation can be crucial for a company's competitiveness when used to increase process efficiency and ultimately reduce operating costs. Second, due to the current configuration of the food system, and several ongoing megatrends as discussed in Chap. 1, the sector needs innovation to overcome the many challenges it faces. Just to mention a few: there is an urgent need to scale up agricultural productivity while reducing impacts on the environment through more efficient use of natural capital; supply chain competitive dynamics should be redesigned and rebalanced to distribute the value produced more fairly among different players, especially farmers; nutrition and health should be put at the center of business concepts in the agribusiness at the global level.

Technological progress, and with it the subsequent development of innovative solutions that can replace less efficient ones, is definitely a lever to achieve these goals. At the same time, it is necessary to assess technological innovations pragmatically, starting from the assumption that they are neither positive nor negative, harmful nor helpful. If adopted consistently with business strategy and processes, disruptive and incremental technological innovations can offer profitable, sustainable opportunities to players in the agribusiness industry.

Moreover, the success of investments in technological innovation depends on the original content of the new product (or service) and its ability to satisfy the expectations of the market. For these reasons, in evaluating the potential of a technological innovation, we must clear away the generalized technology hype and understand the stage of technical development, on the one hand, and the level of acceptance and legitimacy that it would receive from the market, on the other.

This way of looking at technological innovations fits with the technological innovation systems (TIS) research stream. TIS are socio-technical systems focused on the development, diffusion, and use of a particular technology in society (Bergek et al., 2007). In line with these studies, we believe that this development and diffusion cannot be entirely explained by considering individual firms. Novel technologies, especially when they clash with established social rules and practices and differ considerably from dominant technologies, face difficulties in market uptake due to strong skepticism and little societal legitimacy. At the same time, it has been demonstrated that institutions, through regulations and financial incentives, play a crucial role in enabling novel and disruptive technologies to overcome such barriers.

Applying this approach to the study of technological innovations, in this chapter we provide a detailed analysis of innovation in the agribusiness sector, starting from the results outlined in Chap. 1. To remind readers, we are referring to 8 trends, 22 applications, and 47 technologies that together represent an updated overview of technological innovation in the industry. More specifically, Section 2.2 presents the distribution of the innovations in question along the entire agribusiness supply chain and discusses their ability to respond to the challenges of the sector. We assume that the success of each innovation will depend on its ability to meet the needs arising from specific challenges. Section 2.3 presents an assessment of the potential for technological innovations in the agribusiness industry, examining both the technical aspects and the external factors that influence their dissemination and success as business concepts, including social legitimacy and regulatory support. Finally, we offer some takeaways concerning the most promising areas for investors who are at the intersection of the agribusiness and the infrastructure sectors.

## 2.2 The Agribusiness Innovation Landscape: Who Is Innovating and Why?

### *2.2.1 Dissecting Technological Innovations in the Agribusiness Industry*

As anticipated in Chap. 1, given the scope of technology and innovation, studying these concepts requires a structured approach with clear definitions and classifications. The need for a robust methodology also stems from the multifaceted nature of technological innovations. In fact, they exert a multi-layered impact on agribusiness. On the one hand, they provoke changes at the product, process, and business model levels; on the other, they span different links in the value chain. The categorization made in the previous chapter using the DEVO Lab HIT Radar Taxonomy (see Sect. 1.4) provided a valuable starting point for analyzing each technological innovation.

As a first step, we examined the technological innovations in question to define the players in the agribusiness supply chain who might sell or adopt them, providing an intuitive overview of all the interested players. To this end, the selected innovations were also reviewed under the lens of the classification as a product, process, or business model innovation.

- A product innovation is the introduction of a good or service that is either new or significantly improved in terms of its characteristics or intended uses, with the aim of fulfilling a user need. This can include enhancements in technical specifications, materials, software, user-friendliness, or other functional features (OECD, 2015).
- A process innovation is the implementation of a new or significantly improved production or delivery method to decrease unit costs of production or delivery, to increase quality, or to produce or deliver new or significantly improved products/services. This includes major changes in sources of supply, production techniques, and equipment and/or software delivery methods (OECD, 2015).
- Business model innovation is the application of a new business model in an industry: both new companies and established firms can introduce this type of innovation (Amit & Zott, 2012).

Secondly, we analyzed each technological innovation qualitatively to investigate its ability to respond to one or more of the agribusiness industry's challenges as identified in Sect. 1.3.3. These challenges can be seen as objectives that the food system must achieve to become more sustainable and resilient in the long run. They are:

- To increase agriculture productivity and reduce the current inefficiencies related to food loss and waste;
- To use natural resources efficiently, to mitigate agriculture's impacts on the environment, and to restore and enhance ecosystem services;
- To improve public nutrition and health;
- To better distribute value along the supply chain.

Notably, our analysis focused specifically on the application level of the HIT Radar Taxonomy, which involves the combination of technologies for specific purposes. We chose to focus on this level because applications represent an intermediate level that falls between trends and technologies. Trends are too broad to provide a clear target for investments, while technologies can do so only when they are combined in applications that serve a sector-specific purpose.

This approach also lays the foundations for the analysis in Chap. 3, where technological applications are the focal points for examining the agritech-focused private equity and venture capital scene. Applications also inform our discussion of the implications for investors and asset managers at the intersection of the agriculture and infrastructure segments of the alternative asset investment space.

### *2.2.2 Distribution of Technological Innovations Along the Supply Chain*

To better understand the players that are involved in the process of innovation and value creation in the agribusiness supply chain, Table 2.1 presents an outline of each supply chain stage. Specifically:

- the largest players;
- the market size, level of concentration, and compound annual growth rate (CAGR);
- the dominant competitive dynamics;
- the main growing markets;
- the value-added factors driving growth and innovation.

Data reported in the table do not refer to a specific geographical area; instead, they describe the global food system as a whole. Comparing the information outlined in the table, some relevant characteristics of this sector emerge as regards the players' different levels of concentration, market size, and factors deemed crucial for market growth. In particular, we note that farmers have a market size among the highest, but at the same time they are the players with the lowest market concentration. The result is that farms are very fragmented, and on average small compared to companies operating upstream and downstream of the value chain. However, due to this

**Table 2.1** Agribusiness Supply Chain: Players, Competitive Dynamics, Drivers (Source: AGRI Lab)

| | Players description | Concentration | Largest players | Market size (2020) | CAGR (exp) | Competitive dynamics | Growing markets | Growth drivers |
|---|---|---|---|---|---|---|---|---|
| Service and technology providers | Tractors and farm equipment providers | Mid | Deere & Company, Kubota Corp., CNH Industrial, AGCO Corporation, Mahindra and Mahindra | USD 66.56 bln | 5.8% (2026) | R&D, vertical integration (M&A, partnerships, joint ventures); portfolio proliferation | North America, Asia Pacific | Fuel efficiency, sustainability, "product as a service," platform integration |
| | Farm management software providers (accounting and finance, operations management, weather and market intelligence, input and resources management, compliance) | Low | Deere & Company, Trimble Inc., GEA Group, Raven Industries, Agjunction, Delaval, The Climate Corporation, Iteris Inc., Conservis Corp., Topcon Positioning Systems Inc. | USD 1.2 bln | 14% (2027) | Horizontal integration (M&A, partnerships, joint ventures) | North America | Input efficiency, crop yields, sustainability, farm profitability, service integration |
| Input providers | Seed companies (seed type: transgenic hybrids, non-transgenic hybrids, open-pollinated varieties; crop type: grains and cereals, pulses and oilseeds, commercial crops, fruits and vegetables, other crop types.) | Very high | Bayer Crop Science SE, Syngenta International AG, Corteva AgriScience, Groupe Limagrain, KWS SAAT SE & Co., KGaA | USD 63.0 bln | 6.2% (2026) | R&D, portfolio proliferation, geographical presence, aggressive acquisition strategy | North America, Asia Pacific | Input efficiency, crop yields, sustainability, data collection, and analysis |

(continued)

**Table 2.1** (continued)

| | Players description | Concentration | Largest players | Market size (2020) | CAGR (exp) | Competitive dynamics | Growing markets | Growth drivers |
|---|---|---|---|---|---|---|---|---|
| | Agrochemical companies (pesticides, adjuvants and plant growth regulators; crop-based and non-crop-based) | Low | Bayer Crop Science SE, Adama Agricultural Solutions, Yara International ASA, BASF SE, Corteva AgriScience, Nufarm | USD 61.3 bln | 3.7% (2026) | R&D, portfolio proliferation, horizontal integration (M&A, partnerships, joint ventures) | North America, Asia Pacific | Sustainability and biobased solutions, safety, and effectiveness |
| | Fertilizers Companies (straight and complex fertilizers) | Very high | Yara International ASA, The Mosaic Company, Nutrien Limited, EuroChem Group, PhosAgro, K + S, Aktiengesellschaft, Groupe OCP | USD 171.7 bln | 2.4% (2027) | R&D, portfolio proliferation, geographical presence | Asia Pacific | Environmental constraints and energy costs |
| | Feed industry | Mid/High | New Hope Group, Cargill, Land O'Lakes, Wen's Food Group, Muyuan Foodstuff, BRF, ForFarmers N. V., Tyson Foods, Nutreco | USD 352.9 mln | 3.26% (2027) | Horizontal and vertical integration, R&D, portfolio proliferation | North America, Asia Pacific | Growing livestock population, new ingredients, animal health and welfare, efficiency and sustainability |
| Farmers | Farms (fishing, hunting and trapping, forestry and logging, | Very low | – | USD 4.5 tln (est. at farmgate prices) | 6% (2025) | Large land acquisition, downstream vertical integration | North America, Asia Pacific | Input efficiency, crop yields, sustainability, land investments |

| | | | | | | | | |
|---|---|---|---|---|---|---|---|---|
| | agriculture and forestry services) | | | | | | | profitability, large private investors |
| F&B Industry | Food and Beverage Manufacturers (beer m.; wine m.; spirits m.; coffee and tea m.; soft drinks and ice m.; flour, rice and malt m.; other grain products m.; breakfast cereal m.; sugar and confectionery products m.; bread and bakery products m.; cookies, crackers, pasta, and tortillas m.; perishable prepared food m.; snack food m.; all other miscellaneous food m.; frozen food m.; canned/ambient food m.; milk and butter m.; cheese m.; dry, condensed, and evaporated dairy product m.; ice | Low | Nestlé, PepsiCo Inc., Anheuser-Busch InBev, JBS, Tyson Foods, Archer Daniels Midland Co., Mars, Cargill, The Coca-Cola Co., Kraft Heinz Co, Mondelez International, Smithfield Foods, Suntory, Danone, Olam International, CHS Inc., Heineken, Asahi Group, Unilever, General Mills | USD 6.1 tln | 7% (2023) | R&D, portfolio proliferation, horizontal integration (M&A, partnerships, joint ventures), upstream integration/coordination | North America, Asia Pacific | Natural ingredients, health and nutrition, functional foods, efficiency, sustainability |

(continued)

**Table 2.1** (continued)

| | Players description | Concentration | Largest players | Market size (2020) | CAGR (exp) | Competitive dynamics | Growing markets | Growth drivers |
|---|---|---|---|---|---|---|---|---|
| | cream and frozen desserts m.; meat products m.; poultry m.; seafood m.; flavoring syrup and concentrate m.; seasoning and dressing m.; fats and oils m.; pet food m.; animal food m.; cigarettes, cigars and cigarillos m.; smoking and other tobacco products m.) | | | | | | | |
| | Food processing and handling (processing, packaging and service equipment) | Low | Buhler AG, GEA Group, Alfa Laval, JBT, Tetra Pak, IMA, Welbilt, Krones AG | USD 99.68 bln | 4.3% (2028) | Horizontal and vertical integration, R&D, portfolio proliferation | North America, Asia Pacific | Traceability, food preserving, ready meals packaging, sustainability |
| Distributors | Food and beverage retailers (fixed point-of-sale locations: grocery stores, specialty food stores, convenience stores | Mid/High | Sysco (USA), Couche Tard (Canada), Tesco (UK), Seven & I Holdings, (Japan), Woolworths (Australia), | USD 1.7 tln | 7% (2025) | Geographical footprint expansion, technology and automation | Asia Pacific | Servitization, home delivery, ease of purchase, convenience vs premium |

| | | | | | | | | |
|---|---|---|---|---|---|---|---|---|
| | and beer, wine and liquor stores) | | Wesfarmers (Australia), Royal Ahold Delhaize N.V. (Netherlands), CP All (Thailand), Kroger (USA), AEON, Carrefour, Yonghui Superstores, George Weston, Jeronimo, Martins, Colruyt (Belgium), President Chain Store, Metro (Canada), Sun Art Retail Group, US Foods (USA), X5 Retail Group (Netherlands) | | | | | |
| Delivery services | Online delivery services (restaurant-to-consumer delivery, platform-to-consumer; web, phone, app) | Mid/High | Delivery Hero Holding, Foodpanda, Just Eat Holding, Takeaway, Grubhub, Domino's Pizza, Pizza Hut, Foodler, Deliveroo, Ubereats, McDonalds, Seamless, Subway, Snapfinger, Zomato, Olo, Yemeksepeti, Meituan, Go-Food, Swiggy, Eleme | USD 126.9 bln (2021) | 11.4% (2027) | Geographical footprint expansion, technology and automation | North America, Asia Pacific | Profitability (logistics and labor costs), environmental regulations, labor regulations, delivery speed and ease of order |

configuration, they are at the same time among the players with the greatest potential for change and growth.

Given the agribusiness value chain description offered in Table 2.1, the result of the distribution of innovation along it shows that all points mapped represent product innovations for service and technology providers, revealing this category of players as the key to industry evolution (see Table 2.2).

Proceeding from left to right along the supply chain (i.e., by looking at the matrix of Table 2.2 and starting from the columns on the left and moving to the right), chemistry and biotechnology advances and novel farming systems represent, respectively, process and product innovations for input providers. In particular, the most interesting steps forward concern NBTs for plants, livestock, and fish (see Sect. 1. 4.3), and algae and insect farming, which are capturing the animal feed industry's attention as new sources of supply and more sustainable and protein-rich ingredients for their products (see Sect. 1.4.4).

At the stage of the supply chain that involves farmers, the key process innovations that drive evolution are agricultural technologies, innovative solutions for aquaculture, advances in chemistry and biotechnology, and traceability technologies.

More in detail, the use of robotics and advanced sensors provides support for farmers, particularly in managing farm operations: robots replace humans in field work such as sowing, harvesting, pest detection, and weed removal; drones and satellites can detect crop conditions and soil characteristics from above; decision support systems assist farmers thanks to sensors, data, and climate forecasts. The precision introduced by technologies allows farmers to make targeted use of their main inputs. More specifically, water, fertilizers, pesticides are utilized only where needed and in quantities corresponding to the real needs of the plant. Furthermore, the use of sensors enables real-time monitoring of crop health, for example by controlling the emergence of plant pathogens. This is useful for two reasons: first, to rationalize agronomic practices which, if not well calibrated, could induce pathogenesis in plants; second, to minimize treatments with synthetic chemicals, with direct positive impacts on ecosystems.

As for aquaculture (see Sect. 1.4.5), technological innovation in this field allows farmers to apply control-engineering principles to monitor, regulate, and document biological processes in fish farms to improve fish health, and increase productivity, yield, and environmental sustainability. In particular, digital applications play a crucial role in fish farming. Just to mention a few, computer image analysis can provide a non-invasive method for remote monitoring of the size, shape, and conformation of fish (Ruff et al., 1995), and robotics and Internet of Things (IoT) technologies provide farmers with information regarding water quality (Ravalli et al., 2017) and daily fish feeding (Von Borstel et al., 2013; De Mattos et al., 2016).

Business model innovations at the farm level are mainly related to novel farming systems, such as insect farming, algae farming, vertical farming (see Sect. 1.4.4), and energy-related businesses. For example, as far as the latter are concerned, today farms can innovate and diversify their risk by entering into the business of bioenergy production and intelligent agrivoltaics (see Sect. 1.4.2).

**Table 2.2** Distribution of technological innovations along the agribusiness supply chain (Source: AGRI Lab)

| Trends | Applications | Service and technologies providers | Input providers | Farmers | Manufacturers | | Distributors | Delivery services |
|---|---|---|---|---|---|---|---|---|
| | | | Production | | Processing | Packaging | Distribution | |
| Renewable Energy in Agriculture | Bioenergy production | Product innovation | | New business | | | | |
| | Intelligent agrovoltaics | Product innovation | | New business | | | | |
| | Solar desalination for irrigation | Product innovation | | | | | | |
| Chemistry and biotechnology | New breeding techniques for plants | Product innovation | Process innovation | Process innovation | | | | |
| | New breeding techniques for livestock | Product innovation | Process innovation | Process innovation | | | | |
| | New breeding techniques for fishes | Product innovation | Process innovation | Process innovation | | | | |
| Novel farming systems | Vertical farming | Product innovation | | New business | | | | |
| | Algae farming | Product innovation | Product innovation | New business | Product innovation | | | |
| | Insect farming | Product innovation | Product innovation | New business | Product innovation | | | |
| Innovative aquaculture | Land-based aquaculture | Product innovation | | Process innovation | | | | |
| | Sea-based aquaculture | Product innovation | | Process innovation | | | | |
| | Precision aquaculture | Product innovation | | Process innovation | | | | |
| Agri tech | Fuel efficiency | Product innovation | | Process innovation | | | | |

(continued)

**Table 2.2** (continued)

| Trends | Applications | Service and technologies providers | Input providers | Farmers | Manufacturers | | Distributors | Delivery services |
|---|---|---|---|---|---|---|---|---|
| | | | Production | | Processing | Packaging | Distribution | |
| | Farming automation | Product innovation | | Process innovation | | | | |
| | Data collection and analysis | Product innovation | | Process innovation | | | | |
| Alternative proteins | Cultivated meat, fish, leather, etc. | Product innovation | | | New business | | | |
| | Plant-based products | Product innovation | | | New business | | | |
| | Fermentation-derived protein | Product innovation | | | New business | | | |
| Food safety and traceability | Smart packaging: active, intelligent and connected | Product innovation | | | | Process innovation | | |
| | Food preservation | Product innovation | | | Process innovation | Process innovation | | |
| | Smart traceability | Product innovation | Process innovation | Process innovation | Process innovation | Process innovation | Process innovation | |
| E-commerce | Food delivery ecosystem | Product innovation | | | | | Process innovation | New business |

Moving from farmers to manufacturers, Table 2.2 illustrates that at this point in the value chain, process innovation is embodied by new techniques for food preservation, shelf-life improvement, and smart packaging. Instead, product innovation is represented by novel food which is made by using new ingredients such as algae or insects. In fact, the high perishability of agricultural products, which is a cause of food loss and waste globally, makes shelf life a key issue for growers, manufacturers, and retailers striving to upgrade the sustainability of their activities (see Sect. 1.4.8).

The alternative proteins industry instead represents the main business model innovation at the manufacturer level. Today, the conventional production of meat, eggs, and dairy products at current growth rates is considered unsustainable and inefficient. United Nations scientists state that raising animals for food is "one of the major causes of the world's most pressing environmental problems, including global warming, land degradation, air and water pollution, and loss of biodiversity."[1] The alternative proteins industry (see Sect. 1.4.7) is part of the solution to today's most pressing challenges. Big companies operating in the livestock industry are already entering this promising new segment together with a large number of startups.

At the distributor level, food delivery has emerged as a key industry thanks to the introduction of user-friendly apps and tech-enabled driver networks based on IoT and AI, as well as changing consumer preferences (see Sect. 1.4.9). Early on in the pandemic, lockdowns and physical separation rules gave the sector a huge boost: in the USA, the market has more than doubled during the Covid-19 pandemic and globally food delivery has become a market worth more than $150 billion, more than tripling since 2017. Even though supermarket chains are rapidly organizing to offer delivery to their customers, in most cases startups and companies other than large retailers are launching new businesses based on food delivery.

Lastly, traceability technologies (see Sect. 1.4.8) represent a process innovation that cuts across the entire food supply chain. Traceability has become an increasingly essential element within the modern food system because consumers demand greater food-system transparency to inform their purchase decisions and to reduce food safety risks. At the same time, governments and food agencies need to be more efficient in identifying, isolating, and addressing the sources of food safety issues when they manifest. Moreover, traceability enables supply chain optimization by determining and measuring food loss and supports sustainability goals by measuring the social and environmental footprint of all players involved in food production and distribution.

In conclusion, with the exception of startups in the food delivery ecosystem, what emerges is a lack of technological innovations among retailers and a concentration upstream, among the suppliers of technological solutions and input providers. Most of these innovations are business opportunities or processes innovations for farmers and manufacturers.

---

[1] Steinfeld, H., Gerber, P., Wassenaar, T. D., Castel, V., Rosales, M., Rosales, M., & de Haan, C. (2006). *Livestock's long shadow: environmental issues and options*. FAO.

### 2.2.3 Matching Innovations and Industry Challenges

Qualitatively analyzing the purposes of technological innovations, we can outline five common, fundamental objectives underlying their development:

1. To reduce the impact of human activities on the environment;
2. To increase agricultural productivity;
3. To reduce food loss and waste;
4. To increase agriculture's resilience to climate change;
5. To increase food safety.

However, while some innovations are developed for one specific purpose, others simultaneously pursue multiple goals. The results of our analysis (reported below) show the percentage of applications responding to each previously identified objective.

About 67% of the innovations we identified aim to reduce the impact of human activities on the environment to preserve natural resources and restore ecosystems. In this group of innovations fall the combination of solar energy production with desalination technologies, for example, which contributes to reducing the high energy demand of the growing market of desalination for irrigation. Another example is recirculating aquaculture systems[2] (RAS). In addition to supplying fish in areas affected by water scarcity, these systems can help curb the release of pollutants into the ocean, mitigate the risk of escape of non-indigenous fish, improve fish health through higher water quality and lessen the environmental burden of transport by locating RAS close to suppliers and/or the final market. Hopefully, escalating investments in RAS will boost innovation to minimize relative energy requirements. Other examples are fuel efficiency and farming automation for precision agriculture, which minimize input usage by farmers, and smart traceability, which allows agribusiness supply chain players to monitor food production and transportation environmental performances. Lastly, bioenergy production and agrivoltaics also aim at curtailing the pressure of human activities on ecosystems. Bioenergy puts to good use agricultural biomass waste, replacing more polluting alternative energy sources. Agrivoltaics instead decreases water usage in agriculture thanks to the shade that solar panels create for plants and the consequent condensation.

About 56% of the listed innovations are thought to increase agriculture, meat, and fish farming productivity to ensure food security worldwide. In some cases, technologies optimize conventional processes and products, such as new breeding techniques for plants, livestock, and fish. In others, technologies advance the production of alternative solutions like insect farming. More examples include innovative aquaculture, which leverages controlled environments to optimize fish breeding; or alternative proteins, which might expand the supply of proteins while responding to the need to shrink the environmental footprint of meat production.

[2]Closed controlled systems that constantly recirculate and filter water and that may be placed on land. See Sect. 1.4.5

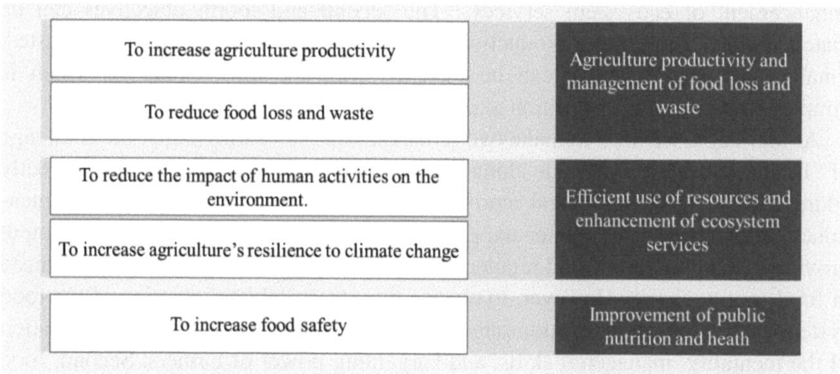


**Fig. 2.1** From innovation objectives to agribusiness industry challenges (Source: AGRI Lab)

About 39% of the mapped innovations aim to curb food loss and waste. Inefficiencies along the supply chain and at the retail level, crop diseases, and the disposal of esthetically unconventional food are just some of the causes of food loss and waste. To tackle these phenomena, some innovations, such as smart traceability, focus on minimizing management inefficiencies; others, such as active packaging and food preservation techniques, directly address food perishability; still others, such as NBTs for plants, intervene on crop resistance to pathogens.

About 33% of the innovations we identified aim to enhance agriculture's resilience to climate change. As natural disasters and extreme weather events become more and more frequent and severe, enhancing food supply resilience is a key goal for the agri-food industry. Indeed, about a third of the mapped innovations are thought to reduce agriculture's dependence on conventional resources. Examples are desalination for irrigation, which exploits seawater to guarantee irrigation services in areas affected by water scarcity; NBTs for plants, which make crops more resilient to extreme climate conditions; vertical farming, which makes it possible to grow plants in a controlled environment, reducing their exposure to natural events; indoor aquaculture, permitting aquaculture in water-scarce regions or where water basin degradation has led to diminished fish stocks; and data collection and analysis, which allow farmers to make more prompt and precise interventions on crops as needed, and to match their agriculture practices with climate forecasts.

About 28% of the listed innovations help increase food safety to improve nutrition and public health. Examples are RAS, which can improve fish health and consequently food safety; smart packaging, to communicate ingredients and nutritional values to raise consumer awareness, or to monitor food conditions to slow spoilage; food preservation techniques deployed during food processing to extend product shelf life; and smart traceability, which means mapping food origin, production steps and transportation, and to monitor food conditions.

These five objectives can be easily traced back to the four challenges characterizing the agribusiness industry (see Fig. 2.1). More in detail, the first and the third objectives can be matched with the challenge of "Efficient use of resources and enhancement of ecosystem services." The second and fourth objectives can be matched with "Agriculture productivity and management of food loss and waste." Finally, the fifth objective can be matched with the third challenge which is "Improvement of public nutrition and health."

At this stage, we need to make two remarks. First, not surprisingly, the challenge of "Better distribution of value along the supply chain" is the only one not directly addressed by the technological innovations we identified. As we previously mentioned, due to their size, intellectual property, and location advantage, it is the input providers, manufacturers, and retailers who hold most of the value-added produced in food supply chains. However, to change this structural configuration of the food system, technological innovations are not enough. What's needed is a transformation of the mentality, managerial skills, and bargaining power of farmers. Second, food delivery represents the only innovation that does not address any urgent challenge, as it is mainly an answer to modern consumers' work–life imbalances and demand for convenience.

## 2.3 Technical and Business Development of Agribusiness Innovations and Implications for Investors

### *2.3.1 Assessing the Potential of Technological Innovations*

The development and diffusion of technological innovations in society and their success as business concepts and/or models depend first and foremost on their ability to satisfy a specific need. In answering to consumers' needs or in an attempt to emerge a hidden need, innovations cannot be valuable from a technical standpoint alone; instead, they must overcome skepticism and gain societal legitimacy. Moreover, the spread of innovations is strictly connected to rules, laws, regulations, and financial incentives, which overall can support or hinder them.

This element is of crucial importance from the point of view of investors and asset managers, who need to carefully weigh the innovative force of a novel technological application against its acceptance and legitimacy in society and among policymakers. The point here is to avoid the risk of regulatory bans or retaliation.

To clear the field of generalized technology hype and identify the most promising areas for investors, we analyze in this section the stage of technical and business development on the one hand, and the level of acceptance and legitimacy that innovations receive from the market on the other. The first dimension captures the technological risk embedded in the proposed applications, while the latter outlines the potential regulatory or societal red flags that may undermine their investment case.

The analysis is focused on the technological innovation that we previously mapped (see Sect. 1.4). More specifically, to conduct this part of our research we interviewed different kinds of experts—practitioners, academics, industry representatives, and consultants—to gather the testimonies of people who study these technologies or have invested in them as entrepreneurs.[3] Our interviews delved deeper into the application level, as this was unanimously deemed to be the most interesting from an investment perspective. The only exception was made for innovative aquaculture and agritech, which we investigated at the trend level. The reasoning here was that, according to our experts, applications encompassed by these two trends are strictly intertwined and, therefore, their relevance can be better understood if jointly analyzed.

We interviewed our experts on the following aspects:

First, we asked them to provide a basic definition of the application in question. If this definition covered a cluster of technologies and/or techniques, we asked them to specify and focus on the most promising one.

Second, we had them illustrate the level of development of the application from a technical and business perspective, highlighting possible areas for further improvement and expansion. We then traced back our experts' responses to two five-point Likert scales (i.e., technical development and business development), following Branscomb and Auerswald (2002). More in detail, from a technical perspective, we considered the following stages of development:

1. Basic research activities: during this phase technical devices or processes with innovative features are developed;
2. Proof-of-concept: this demonstration phase serves to verify the unique commercial value or basic research results;
3. Early-stage technology: this stage involves the validation of how the invention features can fit a target market; production processes are demonstrated, and costs are estimated;
4. Product development: the new technology has successfully entered the market and represents an innovation, but it is still subject to continuous improvements;
5. Technology maturity: there is no room or need for incremental innovation in the technology.

The final score representing the innovation's technical development ranges from basic research (+1) to technology maturity (+5).

From a business perspective, we considered the following five stages of development:

1. Patent: the technology resulting from basic research activities is protected by a patent;
2. Invention: a commercially promising product or service idea is based on new science or technology that is protectable;
3. Business validation: the business case based on the invention can be validated and might begin to attract certain levels of capital;

[3] Interviews were carried out from January to April 2022 and involved a total of 17 experts from Europe and the USA.

4. Innovation: a new science or technology-based product successfully enters into a particular market;
5. Viable business: the business is viable; a standard has been established in the sense that one technology has imposed itself on the others and investors can expect more stable returns on their investments.

The final score representing the innovation's business development ranges from patent (+1) to viable business (+5).

Third, the focus was shifted on the application legitimacy derived from stakeholders, in terms of both public understanding of the working principles of the application and public discourse in support or opposition to it. More in detail, technology legitimacy was split into four types, as per the literature (Jansma et al., 2019): (i) cognitive legitimacy describes the spread of knowledge regarding a technological innovation to the social audience; (ii) normative legitimacy regards judgments about whether an innovation is right for society; (iii) pragmatic legitimacy describes the utility that a technological innovation has for its potential adopters; (iv) regulatory legitimacy concerns the alignment of new practices with existing rules, laws, and regulations issued by governments, credential associations, professional bodies, or powerful organizations.

Experts' responses on each legitimacy component were then traced back to a three-point Likert scale, ranging from absent (−1) to full legitimacy (+1), with neutrality at (0). The final score representing innovation legitimacy is calculated as the sum of each component, which ranges from −4 to +4.

Finally, two qualitative questions were asked to investigate the key elements to be monitored as crucial to the innovation's success as a business concept and its potential development in the next ten years.

The complete survey is reported below, using the insect farming application as an example (Table 2.3).

## 2.3.2 *The Status of Technological Innovations in the Industry*

Figure 2.2 describes the status of innovation in the agribusiness industry considering the technical and business development of technologies. The size of the symbols represents the number of technologies that are placed at a certain intersection of the graph. For example, the big circle with the number 9 inside tells us that 9 out of the 18 innovations have a score equal to 4 for both technical and business development. Instead, the symbols' positions represent the maturity of the innovation in question. The further toward the upper right corner of the graph, the more mature the technologies are from a technical and business perspective.

Overall, the chart shows that innovation in the agribusiness industry is driven both by technologies that have successfully entered the market but are still subject to continuous improvements and by viable businesses. Invention-level innovations, technically at a proof-of-concept stage, are rarer. What's more, they tend to represent

**Table 2.3** Complete text of the survey: The case of insect farming

| | Open questions | Multiple-choice questions |
|---|---|---|
| Definition | How would you define insect farming? | – |
| | If you mentioned more than one technology, which is the most promising and why? | – |
| Technology stage[a] | From a technical perspective, what is the level of development of insect farming? | Given the previous question, please, select one of the following answers:<br>Basic research (1)<br>Proof of concept/invention (2)<br>Early-stage technology development (3)<br>Product development (4)<br>Mature technology (5) |
| | Do you think the innovativeness of insect farming relies in its building blocks or in its architecture? | – |
| Innovation stage[a] | From a business perspective, what is the level of development of insect farming? | Given the previous question, please, select one of the following answers:<br>Patent (1)<br>Invention: functional (2)<br>Business validation (3)<br>Innovation: new firm or program (4)<br>Viable business (5) |
| Technology legitimacy[b,c] | Is insect farming legitimated in public discourse? If not, why? | Cognitive legitimacy:<br>The social audience lacks understanding/awareness of the technology (−1)<br>The social audience understands the working principles of the technology (0)<br>The social audience considers the technology as embedded in the institutional system, and it is unthinkable to have a system without it (1)<br>Normative legitimacy:<br>Public discourse is led by opponents (−1)<br>Public discourse is neutral (0)<br>Public discourse is led by supporters (1)<br>Pragmatic legitimacy:<br>The technology is perceived as not valuable and useful (−1)<br>There is no clear positioning among potential adopters on the technology value and usefulness (0)<br>The technology is perceived as valuable and useful (1) |
| Regulatory support[b,c] | What is public institutions' attitude towards insect farming? | Regulatory legitimacy:<br>Rules, laws, and regulations are adverse to the technology (-1) |

(continued)

**Table 2.3** (continued)

| | Open questions | Multiple-choice questions |
|---|---|---|
| | | There are no rules, laws and regulations on the technology (regulatory gap) (0)<br>Rules, laws, and regulations are in favour of the technology (1) |
| Additional insights | How do you see this technology/business in 10 years from now? | – |
| | Could you mention one or more key elements to be monitored as crucial to insect farming success? | – |

[a]Joseph P. Lane. Understanding technology transfer. Assistive Technology, 11(1):1–19, 1999
[b]Sikke R. Jansma, Jordy F. Gosselt, Kimberly Kuipers & Menno D.T. de Jong Jansma et al. (2019): Technology legitimation in the public discourse: applying the pillars of legitimacy on GM food, Technology Analysis & Strategic Management
[c]Answer by areas if necessary: Europe, North America

a branch of technologies and know-how that has already been developed in other sectors and/or businesses, such as NBTs for fish and fermentation-derived proteins. Others still need improvements from a technical standpoint. For example, indoor, controlled insect farming is an early-stage technology. With a few exceptions in terms of companies breeding insects on a large scale, today the market is made of a few startups that patent their technology and seek funds to develop their operations. The main improvements that we can expect regard process efficiency, feed formulations, and biomass sources to optimize insect farming.

Similarly, for vertical farming technology, there is room for further progress. Current studies focus mainly on LED as illumination, which accounts for the biggest cost item for vertical farms. Other crucial fields of research include plant species-specific treatments and internal logistics optimization. Currently, few vertical farms have achieved economic sustainability or sell their products on the market. Nonetheless, market operators are very interested in this business due to its characteristics of continued availability and full product traceability. Moreover, the pharmaceutical and cosmetic industries also represent potential markets for vertical farm production.

Other innovations whose diffusion is linked with progress in R&D are cultivated meat and fermentation-derived proteins. In particular, for the former, significant advances are expected in four key areas: cell lines, cell culture media, bioprocess design, and scaffolding. Improvements in these domains are crucial to scale up production to significantly larger facilities than what currently exists. As for now, the market is primarily made up of companies (startups or new business lines in companies that operate in the life sciences) trying to find investors and transitioning to pilot-scale facilities.

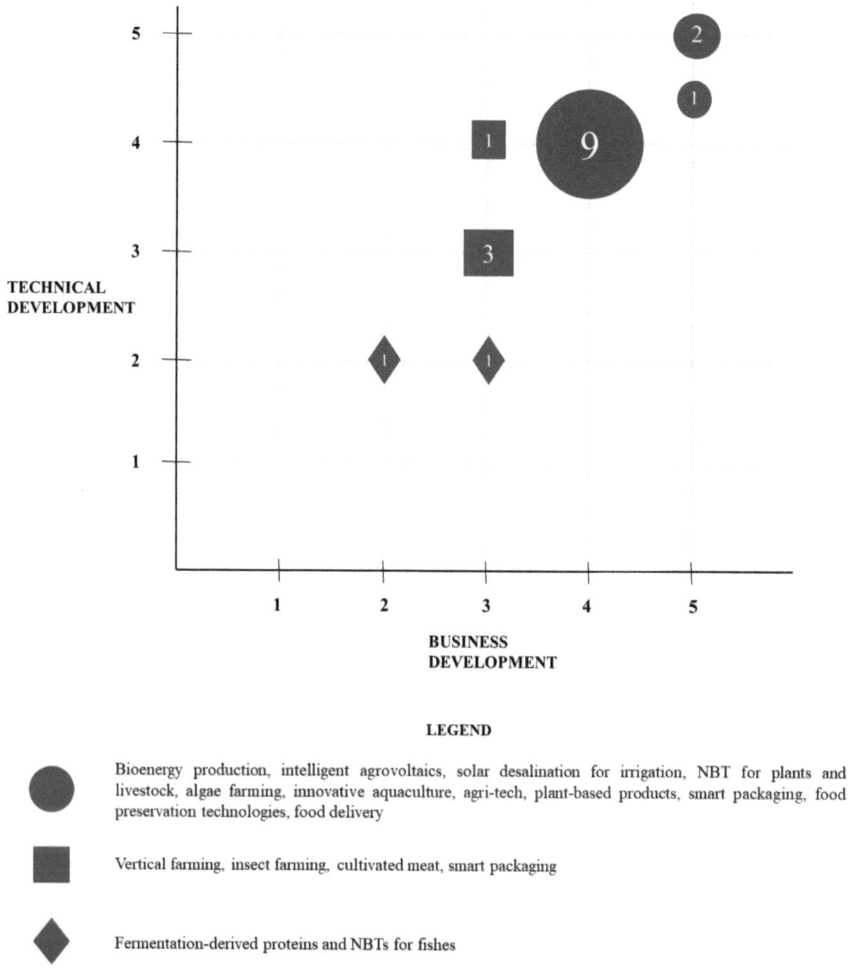


**Fig. 2.2** Technical and business development of innovations (Source: AGRI Lab)

Instead, in the fermentation-derived proteins industry, which represents a subsector of the larger alternative proteins industry, there is room for technological development in the following areas:

- upstream through feedstock optimization and innovation in strain engineering;
- at the level of operations through bioreactor innovation to create equipment that is optimized for food-grade fermentation;
- downstream through advances in processing technologies such as molecule purification or cell harvesting.

Overall, fermentation-derived proteins are entering the proof-of-concept stage, with pioneering products starting to reach customers. This phase will provide

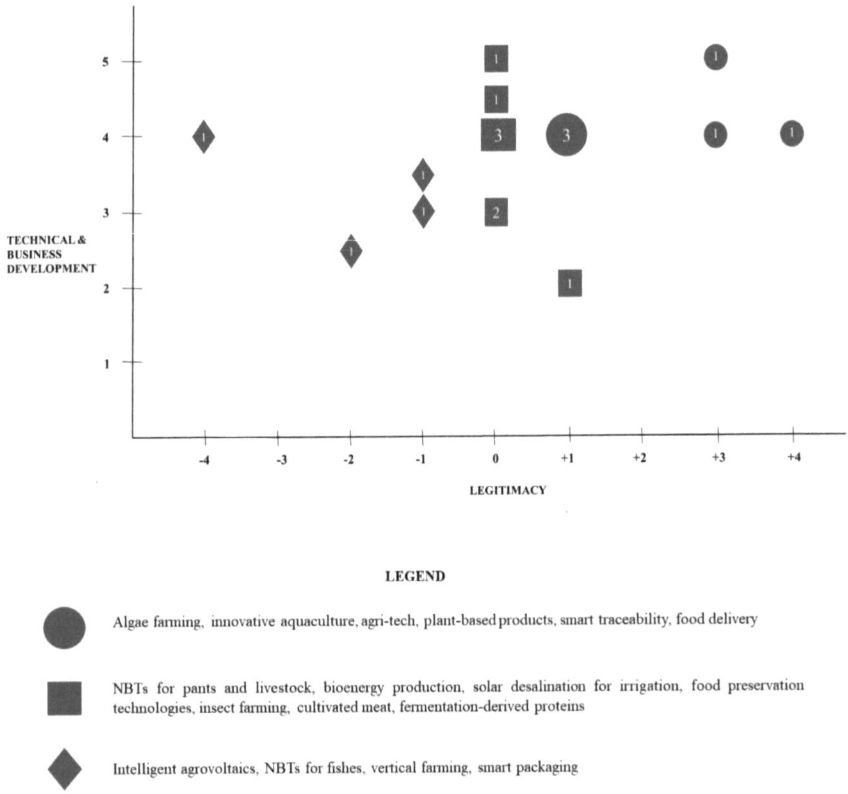


**Fig. 2.3** Technical and business development *vs* legitimacy of innovations (Source: AGRI Lab)

evidence of product-market fit and will help startups in the field refine their product formulations. The key challenge for industry operators is to broaden the range of ingredients to address consumer demand in terms of taste and texture while reducing the unit cost of production of these items. From a market perspective, this industry is a niche when compared to traditional food companies, but it is constantly growing. The majority of B2B companies use this technology to produce alternative proteins supply ingredients that are key to B2C companies, which operate in the plant-based or cultivated meat industries, to improve their final products.

Figure 2.3 represents innovations mapped by the legitimacy (on the *x*-axis), and the technical/business development jointly considered and calculated as the average score of technical development, on the one hand, and business development, on the other·(on the *y*-axis). The result is a picture of the likelihood of adoption and diffusion of technological innovations, consequently highlighting which investment areas are potentially most interesting for investors in the agricultural and infrastructure sector.

We can identify three main clusters of technologies. The first (represented by circles) includes algae farming, innovative aquaculture, agritech, plant-based products, smart traceability, and food delivery. Here we delineate technological innovations that have successfully entered the market and, at the same time, benefit from widespread legitimacy.

The three technological innovations with the highest legitimacy are smart traceability, food delivery, and plant-based products. All are widely known, understood, and accepted by the public; they are considered useful by sector operators, and they are supported (or at least not hindered) by the relative regulatory framework. Consistently with their popularity, these technologies are at a good stage of technical and commercial development, meaning that they are on track to become viable businesses.

Algae farming, agricultural technologies, and innovative aquaculture instead represent technologies with high technical and commercial development and quite good but not full legitimacy. The latter suffers from a lack of cognitive legitimacy, meaning that the public's understanding of these technological innovations is low. Overall, we can observe that cognitive legitimacy is rare for almost all the innovations we identified.

The second cluster (represented by squares) consists of NBTs for plants and livestock, bioenergy production, solar desalination for irrigation, food preservation technologies, insect farming, cultivated meat, and fermentation-derived proteins. In this case, the squares signify technologies that have a low level of legitimacy among the general public or are limited by a regulatory gap. NBTs for plants, for example, have great potential limited by the global regulatory framework. In fact, continuous advancements in the area of plant biotechnology over the last ten years have led to the widespread availability of NBTs that are not yet clearly defined in current Genetically Modified Organisms (GMO) regulatory frameworks. At the same time, countries with a clear normative positioning coexist with others such as the EU and China, which still do not have such a framework. Therefore, uncertainty concerning the regulatory status of the products of NBTs remains a major obstacle to their commercialization (Seyran & Craig, 2018).

Similarly, insect farming development can be hampered by evolving rules. Just to offer an example, we can mention the latest changes in Europe's regulatory framework: on the one hand, in 2017 several species of insects were authorized to be used as feed in livestock. But at the same time, there are still regulatory gaps and restrictive rules, like the one that prohibits feeding larvae with organic waste. Therefore, entrepreneurs in this sector report a feeling of uncertainty about the future direction of relevant rules and, more generally, of the business.

On the other hand, there are technologies such as bioenergy production, NBTs for livestock, and food preservation techniques that are supported by legislation but hindered by public concern for issues relating to health, ecology, and animal rights, as well as not-in-my-backyard attitudes. Food treatment techniques, for example, may encounter public opposition as they could be perceived as affecting the natural characteristics of food and threatening human health. In fact, consumers respond more positively to techniques that are presented as enhancing food's nutritional values and preserving fresh food's positive features.

Lastly, while the proliferation of innovations such as cultivated meat and fermentation-derived proteins is still limited by a lack of cognitive and normative legitimacy, they are highly promising in light of the challenge of food security that they can address.

The third cluster (represented by rhombuses) covers intelligent agrivoltaics, NBTs for fish, vertical farming, and smart packaging and corresponds to technologies that suffer from a lack of legitimacy coupled with scant progress from a technical and commercial standpoint. If we look at intelligent agrivoltaics, for example, we can observe that this technology is short on legitimacy. Although traditional photovoltaic panels are a mature technology, and they are quite common, intelligent systems are still rare. The main cause for the current situation is that even if there is abundant public funding, the relative subsidies do not require synergy between crops and energy production. As a result, farmers opt more frequently for less advanced agrivoltaic solutions. In addition to a clear lack of pragmatic legitimacy, this technology triggers local community protests concerning the esthetic damage to the natural landscape. Lastly, there is an overall regulatory gap concerning these innovative systems. In fact, in many States, current legislation only broadly addresses agrivoltaics, without setting down a clear definition of the systems covered by this label.

### 2.3.3 *Looking Forward: Perspectives Ten Years from Now*

All technological trends and applications under analysis are expected to grow in the coming years, especially as the industry challenges that they address will become ever more urgent. However, their success is still dependent on different factors that mainly concern further technological and scientific advances to enhance their efficiency and reduce their costs, the design of innovative business models to enable their large-scale deployment, normative support, and acceptance by value-chain operators and consumers alike.

Four major clusters of technologies can be identified according to their expected diffusion in the next ten years and the key enabling factors (Fig. 2.4).

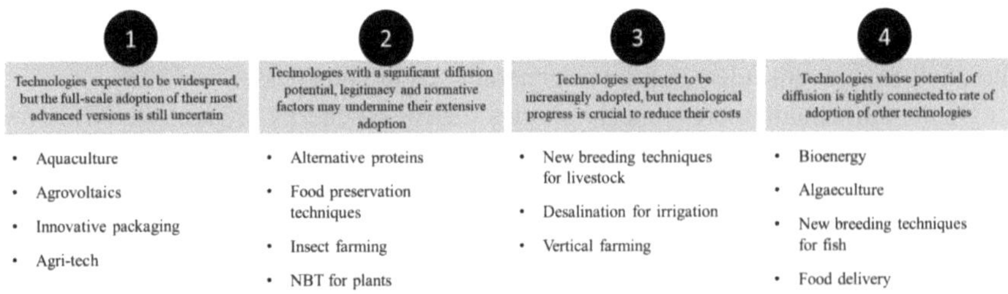


**Fig. 2.4** The four clusters (Source: AGRI Lab)

Some applications are expected to be widespread within the next ten years, but the full-scale adoption of their most advanced versions is still uncertain. These are mainly technologies that are already well-established and at least partially embedded in consumers' and operators' lifestyles. Examples are aquaculture, agrivoltaics, innovative packaging, and agritech. However, their current diffusion does not concern the most upgraded technologies available for each innovation. For example, although aquaculture has a long history, indoor precision aquaculture equipped with RAS is not yet common, and further technological advances would be needed to enhance efficiency and cut costs before we see large-scale adoption. In the field of innovative packaging, on the one hand, biodegradable materials are becoming increasingly common, also spurred on by consumer pressure on industry operators for more sustainable packaging solutions.

On the other hand, smart (active, intelligent, and connected) packaging adoption is still limited as costs are still higher than conventional alternatives and norms in many countries are still restrictive as far as the list of materials that can be adopted to produce food packaging. All this is curtailing further technological advances. Moreover, consumers are mostly unaware of the potentialities of these technologies and are not pressuring industry operators to adopt them, assuaging the sense of urgency. Finally, agricultural technologies, including fuel efficiency, farm automation, and data collection and analysis, are already embedded in the activities of bigger companies. But the lack of connectivity infrastructure, the high cost of technologies, the scarce skills and know-how of the labor force, and the limited interoperability of tools still hinder the full-scale adoption of this cluster of technologies.

While not yet widespread, other technologies have a significant diffusion potential, but legitimacy and normative factors may undermine their extensive adoption, confining some of them to niche markets. For example, the costs of alternative proteins have sharply fallen in the last few years due to technological advances, but their diffusion will require a shift in the dietary preferences of a large portion of the population. If we focus on plant-based products, for example, many experts consider the recent stagnation of this segment as a consequence of the failure to imitate meat adequately, and more generally their inability to meet consumer demand in terms of taste and texture. However, there is heightening attention to healthy diets, more awareness about the need to reduce the pressure on the environment from meat production, and greater concern for animal health. All this will support the spread of innovative products with improved organoleptic properties and nutritional values.

Similarly, food preservation techniques have significantly matured due to intense research and development activities. However, normative restrictions on natural additives and consumer distrust of chemical treatments (mainly driven by little understanding of their working principles) lower their rate of diffusion. An evolution of applicable norms would enhance also the dissemination of new breeding techniques for plants. Indeed, although mature from a technical point of view, dedicated and harmonized laws are lacking, and compliance requirements of the GMO regulations are prohibitive. One consequence of this is that European breeders are cut off from scientific progress, and along with farmers, processors, traders, and consumers, they are at a competitive disadvantage with respect to regions with more conducive regulations. Finally, although the success of insect farming still requires further technological advances, the major barrier to its diffusion is represented by consumers' reluctance; this is confirmed by the more optimistic forecasts about the role of insect farming in feed production.

Other technologies are expected to be adopted more widely, but technological progress is crucial to reduce their costs. For example, new breeding techniques for livestock are expected to be widely adopted once technological developments will make them less expensive. Some other applications whose costs are still not competitive with alternative technologies will be primarily diffused in areas with specific needs. For example, while desalination for irrigation has still high costs mainly driven by its energy requirements and its large-scale diffusion would need significant advances in terms of process efficiency, it is already attracting significant investments in regions where water scarcity is particularly compelling and makes alternative solutions less competitive. Similarly, due to its high energy costs, vertical farming will be mainly adopted in urban and desertic areas, where the demand for locally-produced food is on the rise and the need to optimize the areas dedicated to food production is more urgent.

Finally, there are some technologies whose potential diffusion is tightly connected to the rate of adoption of other alternative or complementary technologies. To give some examples, the future of algae culture is linked to the success of alternative technologies. The diffusion of biofuels derived from algae might be hindered by public subsidies for electric vehicles. Similarly, the adoption of biofuels derived from agricultural biomass will be influenced by the applicability of hydrogen and batteries. Likewise, the further diffusion of bioenergy will be dependent on technical development and cost reduction of carbon capture technologies, which are necessary to reduce bioenergy emissions. On the other hand, the adoption of new breeding techniques for fish is connected to indoor aquaculture and, more specifically, to RAS. Indeed, the latter might be crucial to overcoming current normative restrictions related to the risk of farm fish escaping into local waters, extending the applicability of new breeding techniques beyond those countries with particularly conducive laws. Similarly, although food delivery is increasingly embedded in people's habits, further development of last-mile technologies and application program interfaces will impact its evolution.

To sum up, in most cases, to determine whether or not the applications described above fit the industry's major challenges, the fundamental indicators to consider are technological advances (and consequent costs reduction) and evolutions in normative frameworks to predict future diffusion. In addition to this, consumer legitimacy and more in general public discourse play a major role in determining a technology's success or failure.

## 2.4 Conclusion

This chapter investigates and assesses innovations in the agribusiness sector to provide meaningful takeaways for investors and asset managers that operate at the intersection of infrastructure and agriculture investing. In particular, based on a series of interviews with industry experts, we describe the current status of technological innovation in the agribusiness industry. We also explore the technical and business development of the innovations under investigation and provide a projection of the likelihood of their diffusion in the next few years, taking legitimacy into consideration.

The picture that emerges from the analysis of innovations in the agribusiness industry indicates that:

- There is a lack of technological innovations among retailers and a concentration upstream among the suppliers of technological solutions and input providers. Moreover, most of these innovations represent business opportunities or process innovations for farmers and manufacturers.
- All analyzed innovations, except for food delivery, answer to one or more of the following objectives: (i) to reduce the impact of human activities on the environment; (ii) to increase agricultural productivity; (iii) to reduce food loss and waste; (iv) to increase agriculture's resilience to climate change; and (v) to increase food safety. All these objectives can be traced back to the four main challenges that currently affect the agribusiness industry.
- Innovation in the agribusiness industry is driven by technologies that have successfully entered the market (although they are still subject to continuous improvements) and viable businesses. Invention-level innovations, technically at a proof-of-concept stage, are rarer; they tend to represent a branch of technologies and know-how already developed in other sectors and/or businesses.
- Technological advancements aimed at reducing the final cost of products or services are the key to enhancing the diffusion of many of the innovations we analyzed.
- Legitimacy among consumers and industry operators, together with a stable, conducive regulatory framework is crucial to support the spread of innovations. When these two factors are lacking, the large-scale deployment of technological innovations is limited, regardless of their potential.

## References

Amit, R., & Zott, C. (2012). Creating value through business model innovation. 2012, 53. *MIT Sloan Management Review*.

Bergek, A., Jacobsson, S., & Hekkert, M. (2007). Functions in innovation systems: A framework for analysing energy system dynamics and identifying goals for system-building activities by entrepreneurs and policy makers. In Foxon, T., Kohler, J., & Oughton, C (Eds.), *Innovations for a low carbon economy: Economic, institutional and management approaches*. Cheltenham.

Branscomb, L., & Auerswald, P. E. (2002). Between invention and innovation an analysis of funding for early-stage technology development. *Nist Gcr, 02-841.*

Cantú, S. O., & Zapata, Á. R. P. (2006). ¿Que es la Gestión de la Innovación y la Tecnología (GInnT)? *Journal of Technology Management & Innovation, 1*(2), 64–82.

De Mattos, B. O., Nascimento Filho, E. C. T., Barreto, K. A., Braga, L. G. T., & Fortes-Silva, R. (2016). Self-feeder systems and infrared sensors to evaluate the daily feeding and locomotor rhythms of Pirarucu (Arapaima gigas) cultivated in outdoor tanks. *Aquaculture, 457*, 118–123.

Freeman, C. (1982). *Innovation and long cycles of economic development* (pp. 1–13). Seminário Internacional. Universidade Estadual de Campinas.

Hernandez, L. M. B. (2009). Una revisión de la interpretación económica sobre la innovación. *Journal of Technology Management & Innovation, 4*(4), 139–149.

Jansma, S.R. et al. (2019). Technology legitimation in the public discourse: Applying the pillars of legitimacy on GM food. *Technology Analysis & Strategic Management.*

OECD. (2015). *Oslo Manual. Guidelines for collecting and interpreting innovation data.* OECD.

Ravalli, A., Rossi, C., & Marrazza, G. (2017). Bio-inspired fish robot based on chemical sensors. *Sensors and Actuators B: Chemical, 239*, 325–329.

Rogers, E. M. (2003). *Diffusion of innovations* (5th ed.). The Free Press.

Ruff, B. P., Marchant, J. A., & Frost, A. R. (1995). Fish sizing and monitoring using a stereo image-analysis system applied to fish farming. *Aquacultural Engineering, 14*, 155–173.

Seyran, E., & Craig, W. (2018). *New breeding techniques and their possible regulation.*

Schumpeter, J. A. (1934). *The theory of economic development.* Harvard University Press.

Von Borstel, F. D., Suárez, J., de la Rosa, E., & Gutiérrez, J. (2013). Feeding and water monitoring robot in aquaculture greenhouse. *Industrial Robot, 40*(1), 10–19.

# Chapter 3
# Agriculture as an Asset Class in the Alternative Investments Space

**Stefano Gatti and Carlo Chiarella**

## 3.1 Introduction

Against the backdrop of climate change, rising demand, and evolving dietary preferences, as discussed in Chap. 1, agriculture is called to play a fundamental role in the world food challenge over the coming decades. Because of water scarcity and a severe reduction of arable land, combined with a growing—and wealthier—world population to feed, we need to implement processes, techniques, and innovations that can boost productivity and make better use of scarce resources. This call-to-action gains even more urgency in light of the mounting concerns about food security and logistics posed by the global trade bottlenecks that followed the Covid-19 pandemic and Russia's invasion of Ukraine.

It comes as no surprise then that more and more investors and asset managers have started looking at agriculture as an interesting investment theme, precisely when the industry is undergoing a process of transformation driven by technological innovation. This also holds true for infrastructure investors, for whom agriculture represents an evident departure from core and core plus segments toward pure value-added/opportunistic investments.

In this chapter, we first provide an overview of the status quo of agriculture investing and look at how investors in general are approaching this alternative asset class. Then in the second part of the chapter, we narrow down our analysis to the private equity and venture capital universe focused on technological applications in

S. Gatti (✉)
ANTIN IP Professor of Infrastructure Finance, Department of Finance, Bocconi University, Milan, Italy
e-mail: stefano.gatti@unibocconi.it

C. Chiarella
Department of Finance and Accounting, CUNEF Universidad, Madrid, Spain
e-mail: carlo.chiarella@cunef.edu

 
S. Gatti et al. (eds.), *Agriculture as an Alternative Investment*, Contributions to Finance and Accounting, https://doi.org/10.1007/978-3-031-27918-8_3

agriculture and farming (agritech), exploring it from the perspective of infrastructure investors and asset managers. More specifically, with the technological applications identified in Chap. 2 in mind, we examine agritech as an additional asset class in the infrastructure investment space.

Indeed, as investor appetite for the infrastructure asset class has held strong over the past few years and the dry powder available to infrastructure asset managers has reached record highs, opportunities in core infrastructure have become scarcer and more expensive. According to Preqin (2022b, 2022d, 2022f), the 130 infrastructure funds closed in 2021 raised a record $125 billion of aggregate capital, pushing the total assets under management in this asset class over the $1 trillion mark for the first time. But dry powder is also at record highs: above $300 billion according to the most recent estimates. With $123 billion already raised by 39 funds in the first two quarters of 2022, and another 382 funds in the market targeting $220 billion of additional capital, keeping up with dealmaking to deploy these resources is becoming more and more challenging. As a result, infrastructure investors surveyed by Preqin (2022a) are becoming increasingly concerned about finding good deals at reasonable prices. Excessive asset valuations (39%) and competition for good assets (36%) stand out among investors' top three concerns. So asset managers have to rethink their investment process and investment philosophy, taking a broader, more forward-looking view of infrastructure.

More specifically, as the barriers between infrastructure investment and private equity blur and the two asset classes converge, infrastructure asset managers need to hone their ability to identify new strategies that can ensure a solid, sustainable long-term yield for their investors. To do so, we propose moving from core infrastructure to consider investments in the agriculture landscape where new technologic applications have the best long-term potential to reshape the agricultural supply chain. In other words, this is where the introduction of more technology-savvy and data-driven processes will improve agriculture productivity, food supply, and food safety, reduce inefficiencies, and shrink agriculture's environmental footprint.

The rationale we advance for this move is twofold. First, the approach we propose fits well with infrastructure investors' hunt for long-term sustainable returns that are supported by megatrends, such as the climate and demographic transformations driving demand for new and more efficient agriculture, which came up in Chap. 1. Second, and equally important, a more flexible approach also provides infrastructure investors with greater opportunities to pursue emerging investment themes such as green infrastructure (i.e., sustainable and environmental) and intangible data-powered infrastructure.

The rest of the chapter is organized as follows. In Sect. 3.2 we provide an overview of the status quo of agriculture investment, first with a description of the specific features characterizing the asset class, then introducing a taxonomy of investors, and finally commenting on recent trends in fundraising and investing. Next, in Sect. 3.3 we report the results of our analysis of asset managers and investors and recent transactions in the agritech-focused private equity and venture capital space. Finally, in Sect. 3.4 we conclude by offering our views on the future prospects for agriculture investing and the potential for agritech to become an additional asset class in the infrastructure space.

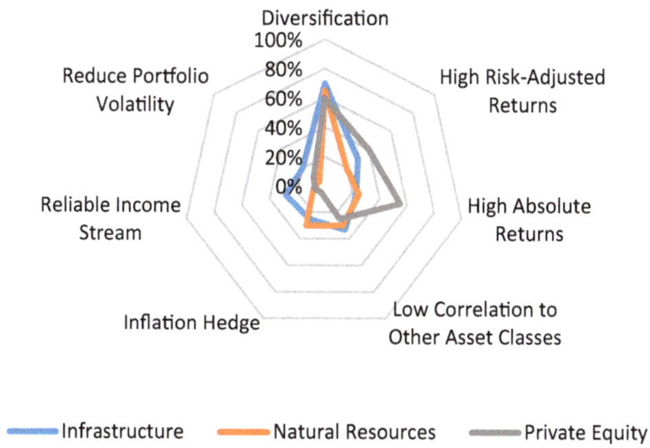


**Fig. 3.1** Institutional investors' main reasons for investing in natural resources (Source: Preqin)

## 3.2 Agriculture Investing

According to the asset management industry's standard definition, the agriculture and farmland asset class typically encompasses the investment of capital into land used for growing crops or raising livestock.[1] This includes the ownership of land, operations and services for livestock and crop production, as well as the technological processes used in agriculture and farming. Historically, from an investor's point of view, agriculture was viewed as an offshoot of the natural resources asset class (also including energy, metals and mining, timberland, and water)[2] which is considered a blend of private equity and infrastructure asset classes (see Fig. 3.1).

On the one hand, a low correlation with other asset classes, rigid and rising global demand, protection against inflation, and resilience to economic downturns are all factors that promise investors in agriculture they will benefit from stable and inflation-linked cash flows for extended periods of time (Alliance Bernstein, 2010; IPE, 2019; UBS, 2020; Sherrick, 2020). On the other hand, however, technological advancements and expanding awareness of the importance of the physical and transition risks related to climate change pose crucial questions for investors and asset managers about the long-term changes that will reshape the established business model of agriculture in the next few years.

Accordingly, the big picture is characterized by the heightened interest in the agriculture asset class among investors. In recent years, positive, continued investor sentiment has been a key contributor to making agriculture a mature, established asset class and engendering greater specialization among asset managers.

[1] See, for example, Preqin Pro Glossary of Terms https://docs.preqin.com/pro/Preqin-Glossary.pdf

[2] Natural resources are materials or substances that occur naturally on Earth. They can be mined, farmed, or collected in raw form. These raw materials are often engineered into more complex manufactured materials and extracted, processed, or refined to realize their economic value.

Indeed, several factors have contributed to piquing interest in the agriculture asset class among investors. These include, for example, the compression of yields that followed the ultra-loose monetary policies put in place by central banks since the Global Financial Crisis through the Great Recession and the recent Covid-19 pandemic. As a result, fundraising for unlisted agriculture has experienced remarkable growth in recent years. Indeed, despite the turbulence brought on by the Covid-19 health emergency and more recently by the outbreak of the armed conflict in eastern Europe between Russia and Ukraine, agriculture has proven to be a resilient asset class, offering investors relatively good yields, also compared to other asset classes. (We will discuss this in more detail in the next subsection.) With the return of inflation, bottlenecks to growth, and possible interest rate hikes posing ever-greater threats to the ability of asset managers to continue offering investors attractive yields, agriculture investments are seen more and more as a safe haven.

In this section, we first highlight the characteristics of agriculture as an asset class in its own right and discuss the risk and return of investing in it. Then we present the elements that have contributed in the recent past to enhancing its appeal to a broader set of investors and asset managers. This leads us to take a closer look at who the most active players are and the most common structures they are using to get exposure to the asset class. More specifically, in an initial attempt to map who invested in what and where, we analyze trends in fundraising and investment in agriculture. Lastly, focusing on the prospects of the asset class in the years to come, we report the amount of dry powder that is yet to be deployed and introduce the outlook for future allocations by managers and investors.

### 3.2.1 Agriculture as an Asset Class

Agriculture has offered investors relatively good yields in recent years. Data reported by Preqin (2022e) indicate that across vintage years from 2009 to 2018, funds targeting agriculture and farmland obtained a median net IRR of 6% with a standard deviation of 8.4%. These performances are comparable on a risk-adjusted basis with those of infrastructure, real estate, and private equity, and well superior to those of other natural resources strategies. (See Fig. 3.2, where the size of the bubbles represents the assets under management.) Moreover, investments within the agriculture and farmland asset class can have different risk/return profiles depending on the process or stage under consideration. In this respect, Preqin separates the traditional landowner and/or operator models that typically achieve notional IRRs in the range between 6–10% from agritech, which exhibits potentially higher returns, of 10% or more at the riskier end of the investment space.

Together with good performances, the climate and demographic changes described in Chap. 1 will put additional pressure on supply and demand for agricultural products; these are also two additional key contributors to a renewed interest in the agriculture asset class among investors. Figure 3.3 shows the results of annual investor surveys conducted by Preqin (2022e) in the first quarter of 2020, 2021, and

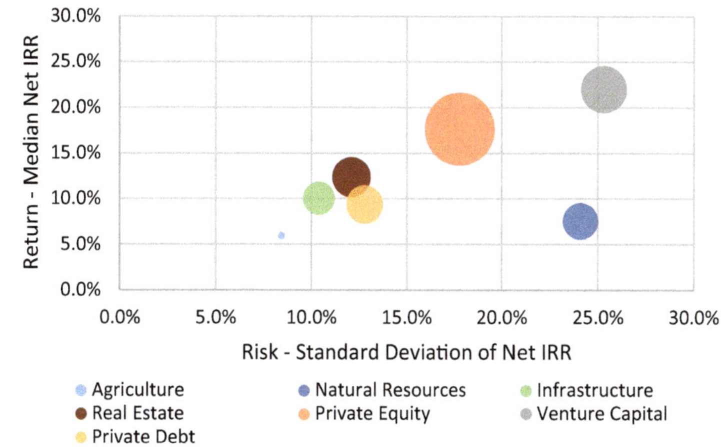


**Fig. 3.2** Risk/return profile of private capital by asset class: vintages 2009–2018 (Source: Preqin)

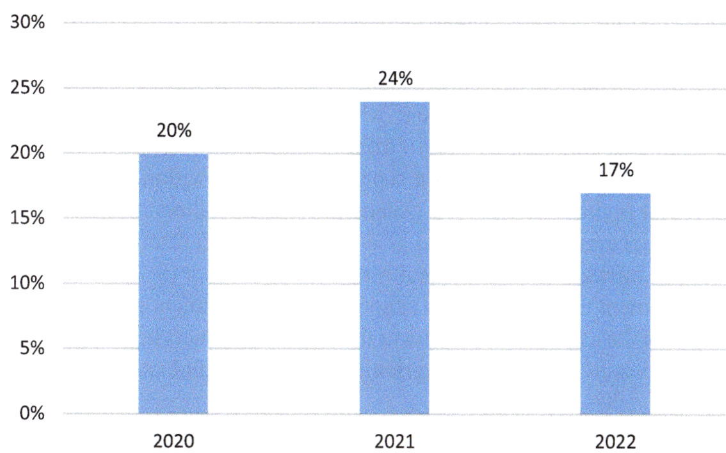


**Fig. 3.3** Strategies targeted to agriculture and farmland by natural resources investors over the next 12 months, Q1 (Source: Preqin)

2022 on their views about different asset classes and the strategies that they will be pursuing over the next 12 months. Consistent with investor appetite being on the rise, about one-fifth of natural-resources investors report that they are specifically targeting agriculture and farmland in this timeframe.

### 3.2.2 A Taxonomy of Agriculture Investors

According to the most recent data compiled by Preqin (2022a), the number of active investors and asset managers in the agriculture and farmland asset class topped 1208 in the first quarter of 2022. These include very different investor types, also in terms of location and investment preference.

Figure 3.4 breaks down agriculture investors by their nationality. North America accounts for 38% of investors, with a large majority from the USA. Asians and Europeans represent 32% and 16%, respectively. Among the former, about half come from China, while another third consists almost equally of Japanese and Indian investors. A large majority of European investors are from Western Europe (53%) or the United Kingdom (30%), with Nordic countries accounting for another 15% and Central and Eastern nations for only 3%. From the rest of the world, Australasian investors represent nearly 5% of the total number of investors, while the share for the Middle East and Africa is about 6%; it is only 2% for Latin America.

Investors' intensifying interest in agriculture is also manifest in the broad spectrum of different investor types that are active in the asset class (see Fig. 3.5): from public and private sector pension plans (17% and 11%, respectively) to family offices (5%), from endowments (13%) and foundations (11%) to government agencies (5%), from banks and investment banks (7%) to investment companies (6%) and fund of fund managers (5%), each one with its own goals and investment horizon. According to data collected by Preqin from institutional investors in 2017, for only 6% of them, agriculture represents a separate allocation within their portfolio. For the majority, it is either part of their general allocation to alternatives (8%) or it falls within their allocations targeting real assets (37%), natural resources (16%), private equity (15%), infrastructure (4%), real estate (4%), or other (9%).

This assortment of investor types echoes in their investment preferences in terms of the stages of the agricultural process or the types of products they target. Figure 3.6 shows the responses to a survey of agriculture investors conducted by Preqin (2016)

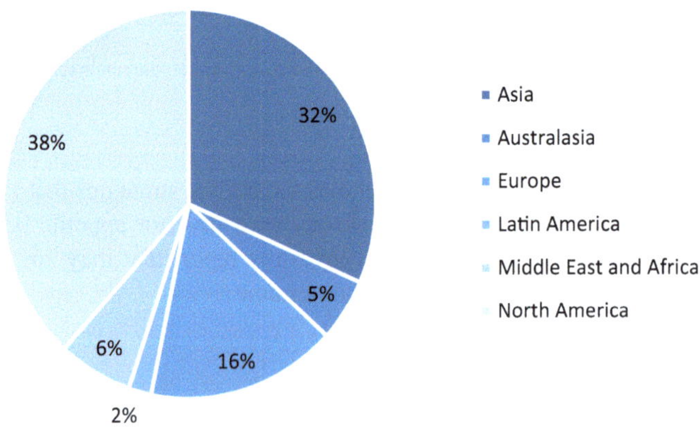


**Fig. 3.4** Active investors in agriculture: breakdown by location (Source: Preqin)

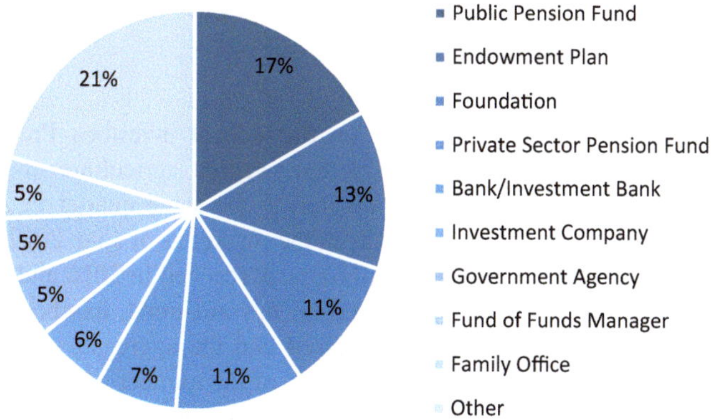


**Fig. 3.5** Active investors in agriculture: breakdown by type (Source: Preqin)

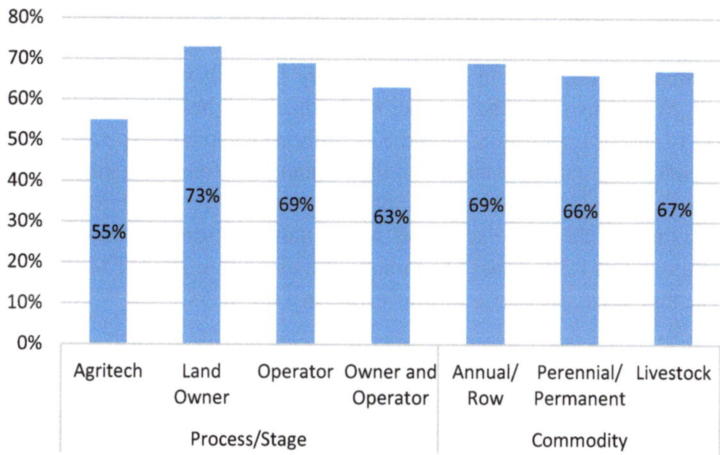


**Fig. 3.6** Active investors in agriculture: breakdown by investment preference (Source: Preqin)

about their investment preferences. Ownership of land is their favorite investment approach, closely followed by investments in operations and services for livestock and crop production. The joint ownership and operation model is less frequent, but still substantial. This can be explained in light of the very different types of risk which investors get exposed to through operation versus ownership, as well as the different skill sets required. Only approximately about one out of two investors indicate agritech as one of their preferred investment strategies, the smallest percentage of all. This suggests that agritech does not appeal to all investors alike, but only to those that have a more specific skill set and the adequate risk/return preferences, as it is perceived as more risky compared to other segments that are easier to value. Regarding the type of agricultural product, there seems to be no clear difference in the frequency with which investors point to annual and permanent crops or livestock among their top targets.

### 3.2.3 *A Map of Fundraising and Investment in the Agriculture Asset Class*

Consistent with the heightened interest on the side of investors, Preqin (2022c, 2022e) recorded 56 funds in the market that targeted agriculture in the second quarter of 2022, up by almost 50% compared to the same quarter in 2016. Still, the aggregate capital targeted by the funds in the market as of June 2022 was about $8.5 billion, falling short of the $12.9 billion peak reached in 2016 and 2017. As a result, the pattern of fundraising, while on an upward trend, has been wayward. Figure 3.7 reports the number of funds closed and the aggregate capital actually raised between 2008 and 2021. A first tidemark of the number of funds closed in a given year was reached in 2013, just after a record fundraising of $4 billion in 2012 and several years of back-to-back growth in both the number of funds closed and aggregate capital raised. Then, while the number of funds closed dropped by almost half in 2015 to just 11, fundraising surged to a record high of $5 billion, suggesting a substantial increase in the average fund size. The peak in the number of funds that closed was 21, reached in 2019, with $3.4 billion raised, as a result of a three-year winning streak starting back in 2017, when only 11 funds were closed for just over $1 billion. Since this peak, the number of funds closed has bounced back to 10 in 2020 and 14 in 2021, raising $2.0 and $2.2 billion of capital, respectively.

This fundraising pattern is similar to that of natural resources in general, to which agriculture and farmland contributed approximately 3% over the period from 2010 to 2021. The share of these two segments within natural resources fundraising ranged from a minimum of 1.5% in 2011 to a maximum of 7.4% in 2017. The average figure was 3.9%, and in excess of 5% in four of the last ten years.

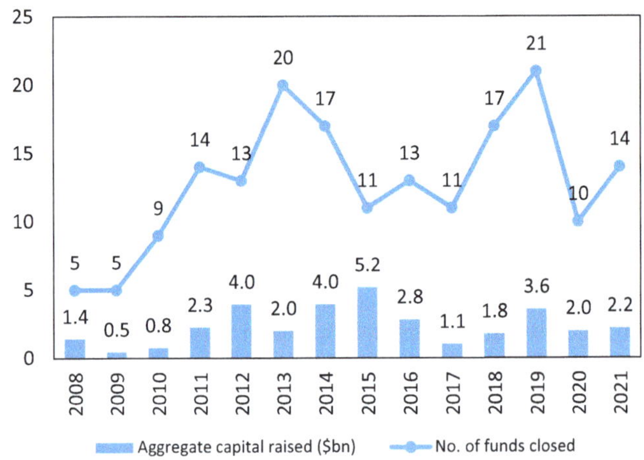


**Fig. 3.7** Annual unlisted agriculture and farmland fundraising: number of funds closed and aggregate capital raised (Source: Preqin)

**Table 3.1** Agriculture and farmland fundraising between 2008 and 2017: number of funds closed and aggregate capital raised by geography

| | Funds closed | Capital raised |
|---|---|---|
| North America | 29% | 37% |
| Asia | 19% | 10% |
| Latin America | 14% | 10% |
| Australasia | 9% | 7% |
| Europe | 5% | 3% |
| Middle East and Africa | 4% | 4% |
| Sub-Saharan Africa | 10% | 3% |
| Diversified | 11% | 24% |

Source: Preqin

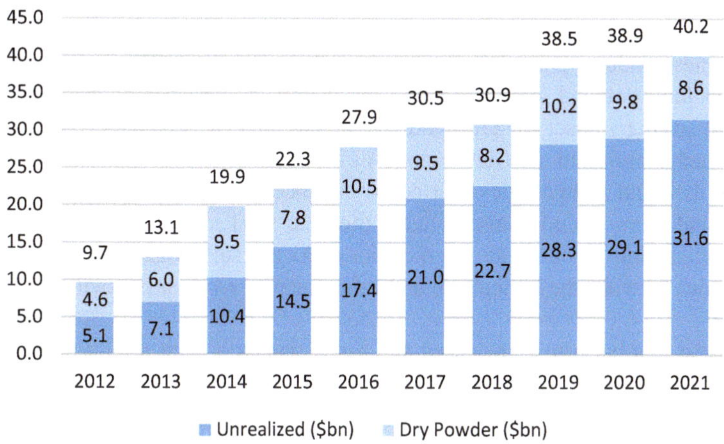


**Fig. 3.8** Unlisted agriculture and farmland assets under management and dry powder (Source: Preqin)

A geographical breakdown of fundraising suggests that the focus of asset managers has been predominantly US- and Asia-centered (Prequin, 2017). According to Table 3.1, of the funds closed between 2008 and 2017, 29% have their primary geographical focus on North America and sum up to 37% of the aggregate capital raised. In addition, 19% of the funds closed in this period and 10% of the capital raised is primarily focused on Asia. Diversified funds represent 11% of the number of funds closed and account for 24% of the capital raised.

Not surprisingly, with both fundraising and investor demand on the rise, assets under management have reached record highs. Figure 3.8 shows that unlisted agriculture fund assets under management have soared more than fourfold since 2012, from about $10 billion to more than $40 billion in 2021. The drawback of such a large flow of capital toward the agriculture asset class is that dry powder has also been piling up, as fund managers are unable to deploy capital in attractive investment opportunities as quickly as they can raise funds. Figure 3.8 shows dry powder has almost doubled since 2012, from $4.6 to $8.6 billion, scoring a record high of $10.5

billion in 2016. According to data collected by Preqin, about half of this pile of unused capital is concentrated in funds focused on North America (43%).

## 3.3 Can Agriculture Become an Asset Class in the Infrastructure Space?

Under the pressure of social and technological disrupting forces, the boundaries between different segments of the private capital ecosystem are rapidly blurring at the aggregate level. On the one hand, infrastructure is not the monolith of the past, nor is it necessarily even a physical asset anymore (see Gatti & Chiarella, 2020). On the other hand, technological innovations and social changes are reshaping the agribusiness industry, as described in detail in Chap. 1. These trends include growing food demand and changes in the dietary preferences of many countries; the intensifying impact on farmland of climate change; water and land scarcity; heightened attention to the GHG emissions of agricultural processes; the emergence of new data and technologies that could enhance process efficiency and improve yields; and more recently, an escalating threat to food security from supply chains interruptions and global trade fragmentation. As a result, what emerges is that the boundaries between the agriculture and infrastructure asset classes will increasingly overlap.

Against this backdrop, investors and asset managers with a long-term horizon, such as those investing in infrastructure, could benefit from embracing a theme investing approach and positioning themselves to exploit the long-term strategic opportunities that are emerging in agriculture. We refer in particular to investing in those products and processes that, with the introduction of new technologies, aim to: (1) improve agriculture productivity and curb food loss and waste; (2) make more efficient and sustainable use of resources; and (3) enhance food security and consolidate/shorten the product supply chain.

Therefore, with the technological applications from Chap. 2 in mind, in this section we investigate the asset managers and investors as well as recent transactions in the agritech-focused private equity and venture capital space. Our analysis starts with an assessment of the status quo of this space and then we move on to discuss future perspectives, describing the implications of the transformative changes ahead for infrastructure investors and asset managers.

### *3.3.1 The Status Quo at the Intersection Between Agriculture and Infrastructure Asset Classes*

To get a sense of the status quo, we begin by analyzing the largest asset managers and investors in the market at the intersection of infrastructure and agriculture, trying to map their approach and their investment styles.

We focus our analysis on the 62 funds recorded in the Agri Investor database that target agritech, with capital raised in excess of $200 million,[3] which corresponds to the top 30% of the distribution of agritech-focused funds. For comparison, consider that depending on the vintage year, infrastructure funds have historically raised on average between $500 million and $1 billion. The oldest vintage year is 2004, but about two-thirds of the funds in our sample were launched in the period 2014–2020. Most of them (56 out of 62) have already reached the final close of fundraising and 50 of them are still currently investing. Their preferred geographic focus is on North America (46.8%), followed by the Asia-Pacific region (32.3%), Middle East and Africa (27.4%), Western Europe (25.8%), Central/Eastern Europe (24.2%), and Latin America (14.5%).

## Asset Managers

Starting from these agritech-focused funds, we define our universe of agritech asset managers based on the general partners (GPs) managing them. Our sample includes 41 GPs, including 19 investment firms, 13 asset management companies, seven corporate or independent firms, and two sovereign wealth funds. Their headquarters are mainly in North America (14) and Western Europe (12). The Asia-Pacific region and the Middle East and Africa region count six each. Another two GPs are based in Latin America and only one each in Central and Eastern Europe.

According to the information available on their corresponding tearsheets, provided by Agri Investor, all these GPs but one indicate agribusiness as one of their preferred target sectors, together with farmland (8), water (2), and timber/forestland (2). Moreover, 39 out of these 41 GPs explicitly list agritech among their favorite allocation strategies in the agriculture investment space.

To get a better picture of the variety of their approaches to agritech investing and their different investment styles, for the GPs in our sample we collected additional information from Capital IQ Pro. More specifically, for each one we merged the information obtained from their tearsheets on Agri Investor with additional input available in the company reports on the Capital IQ Pro platform, based on individual text searches of their names. Table 3.2 reports a summary of descriptive statistics for the GPs in our sample, which we take as representative of the agritech asset management universe as of the end of December 2021.

On average, the GPs in our sample manage approximately three funds for an aggregate value of about $11 billion of assets under management (AUM), suggesting the agritech investment space is populated by mid-sized asset managers, with the largest GP managing $130 billion of assets over 16 funds. These are also experienced asset managers. The average GP counts about eight funds closed and a total of approximately $5 billion of funds raised in the last ten years. The number of active

[3] Overall, the Agri Investor database covers around 1000 funds with a focus on agriculture with vintage years between 1994 and 2022.

**Table 3.2** Agritech asset managers, as of the end of December 2021

| | Obs. | Mean | St. Dev. | Min | Median | Max |
|---|---|---|---|---|---|---|
| Number of funds managed | 41 | 2.76 | 2.65 | 1 | 2 | 16 |
| AUM ($ million) | 20 | 11,227 | 29,294 | 297 | 2406 | 130,000 |
| Total raised (Last 10 years) | 22 | 4984 | 15,681 | 2 | 602 | 73,512 |
| Dry powder ($ million) | 22 | 1349 | 4853 | 0 | 157 | 22,891 |
| Funds in the market | 28 | 0.61 | 1.10 | 0 | 0 | 4 |
| Funds closed | 28 | 7.89 | 16.36 | 0 | 3 | 84 |
| Total active investments | 24 | 67.33 | 179.38 | 1 | 19 | 875 |
| Min bite size ($ million) | 19 | 16 | 31 | 0 | 5 | 129 |
| Max bite size ($ million) | 19 | 233 | 458 | 1 | 50 | 1685 |

Source: authors' elaboration of data provided by Agri Investor and Capital IQ Pro

investments per GP is on average 67, reflecting the typically small average bite size of agritech investments, which range between a minimum mean value of $16 and a maximum of $233 million. The average dry powder per GP is estimated at around $1.3 billion, which suggests an increasingly competitive market for deals.

Only three of the GPs in our sample of agritech asset managers are also ranked among the top 100 global infrastructure fund managers in the annual list produced by Infrastructure Investor, based on the capital raised by infrastructure direct investment programs over a five-year period.[4] In order to investigate more thoroughly the degree to which the agritech asset management universe overlaps with infrastructure, we also collected more qualitative information from Capital IQ Pro on GPs' investment topics and industries of interest, as well as their preferred deal structure type and development stage.

This information allows us to classify GPs across a number of non-mutually exclusive categories based on their investment preferences. As a result, Fig. 3.9 shows the top five recurrent investment topics as well as the top ten industries of interest among the GPs in our sample. Notably, among the most recurrent investment topics among agritech-focused asset managers, we find renewable energy (26.7%), smart energy (20%), and water purification (13.3%), which are some of the typical targets of infrastructure investors.

Other recurring investment topics are more specifically related to agricultural processes such as farming (20%), animal feed (13.3%), and aquaculture (13.3%). Nonetheless, the GPs in our sample report interest in investment opportunities across a broad spectrum of industries. Consistent with a generalist approach, a majority of them cover all major business activities, including consumer products (82.8%), industrials (75.9%), producers (79.5%), commercial and professional services (65.5%), capital goods (62.1%), healthcare (62.1%), materials (62.1%), environmental facilities and services (58.6%), retail (58.6%), and agricultural services (55.2%).

[4]The Infrastructure Investor list of the 100 largest infrastructure fund managers globally by size is available on its web page (http://www.infrastructureinvestor.com)

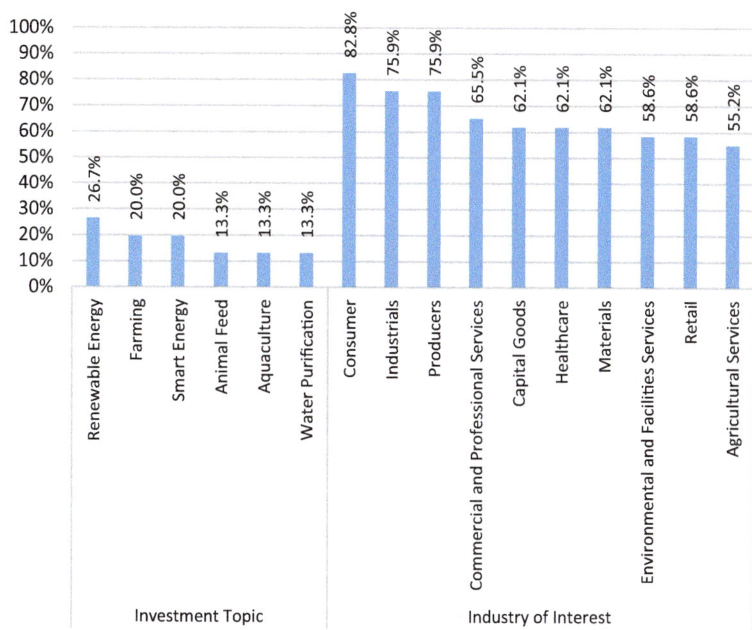


**Fig. 3.9** Investment styles of agritech asset managers: topics and industries of interest (Source: authors' elaboration of data provided by Capital IQ Pro)

The investment preferences of the GPs in our sample, as regards their preferred deal structure and development stage, are reported in Fig. 3.10. The dominant focus in terms of deal structure is on buyout (65.4%) and growth capital (65.4%) strategies. Other structures are much less frequent. Fewer GPs target deals related to industry consolidation (11.5%), mezzanine (7.7%) and bridge (3.8%) finance, and private investments in public equity (3.8%). Moreover, early ventures are the preferred target of a majority of our GPs (59.1%). These are followed by companies that are in the seed or startup stage (45.5%), middle market companies (40.9%), late ventures (36.4%), or turnaround targets (31.8%). Other stages of development attract fewer GPs, such as in the case of incubation (13.6%), mid venture (22.7%), emerging growth (22.7%), mature (13.6%), and later stage (27.3%).

Figure 3.11 shows instead the frequency with which the agritech-focused GPs in our sample indicate an interest in infrastructure-related investment topics or industries. Following Preqin, our definition of infrastructure includes renewable or conventional energy, telecoms, transport, utilities, social, and other infrastructure. We then tag each investment topic or industry of interest that comes up with one of the categories based on EDHECinfra's infrastructure taxonomy.[5] A majority of the GPs

[5]The Infrastructure Company Classification Standard (TICCS) is available at https://edhec.infrastructure.institute/ticcs/ (EDHECinfra, 2022)

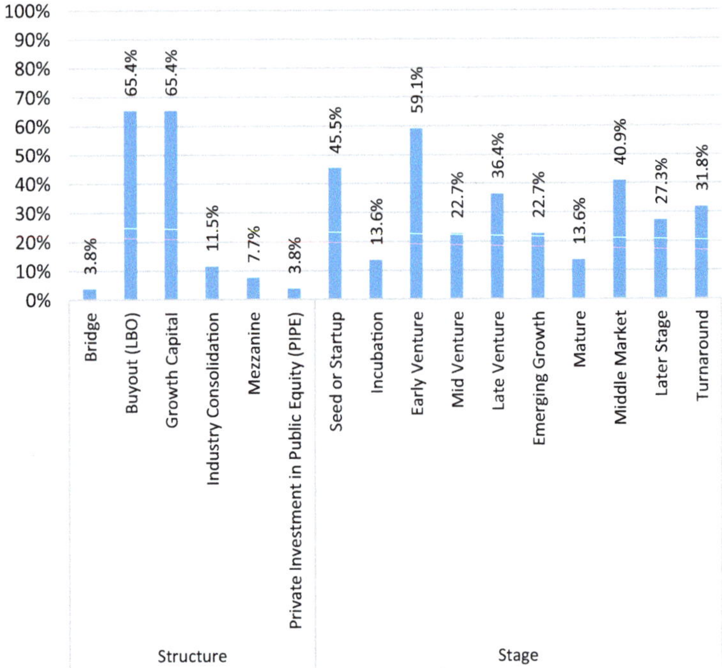


**Fig. 3.10** Investment styles of agritech asset managers: deal structure and development stage (Source: authors' elaboration of data provided by Capital IQ Pro)

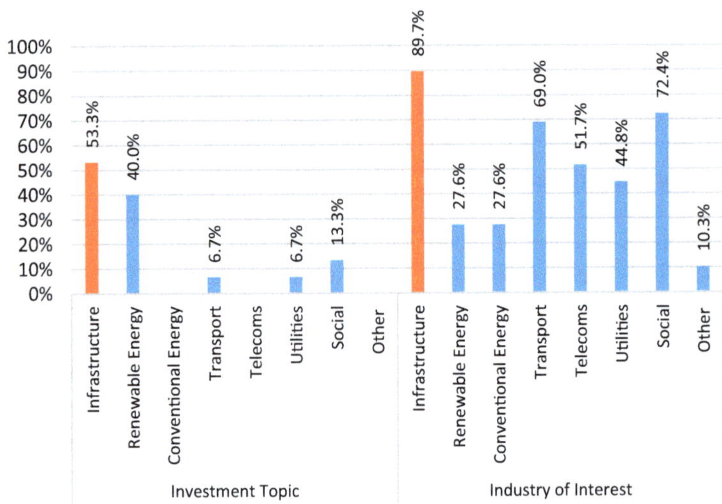


**Fig. 3.11** Agritech asset managers' interest in infrastructure-related investment topics and industries (Source: authors' elaboration of data provided by Capital IQ Pro)

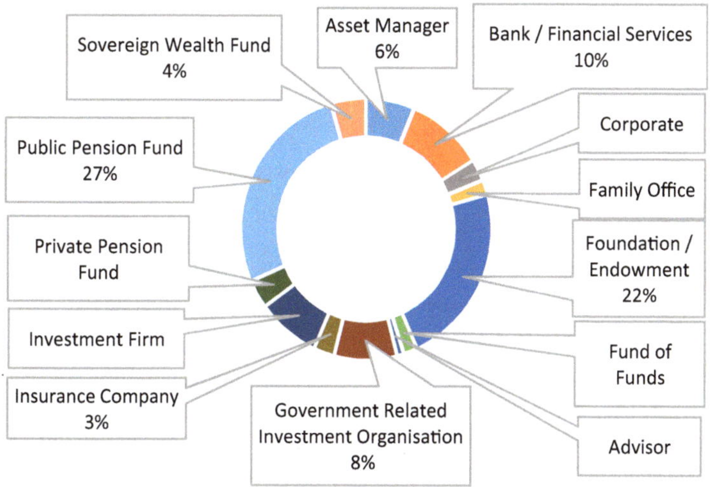


**Fig. 3.12** Agritech investors: sample breakdown by type (Source: authors' elaboration of data provided by Agri Investor)

in our sample (53.3%) express an interest in infrastructure-related investment topics, especially those concerned with renewable energy (40%) but also in the sphere of social infrastructure (13.3%), transport (6.7%), and utilities (6.7%). The interest in infrastructure-related industries is even more generalized. In fact, almost all the GPs in our sample (89.7%) report targeting industries related to renewable or conventional energy (27.6%), telecoms (51.7%), transport (69%), utilities (44.8%), social (72.4%), and other infrastructure (10.3%). This is once again consistent with a generalist approach by the GPs, who are well-positioned to play a pivotal role in helping infrastructure investors to embrace those agriculture investments focused on the innovations in the technological processes used in agriculture and farming, as in the case, for example, of precision farming and data-based farming.

### Investors

We define our universe of agritech investors based on the limited partners (LPs) with funds committed to any of the 62 agritech-focused funds in the Agri Investor database. Our sample includes a well-assorted set of 111 LPs. It comprises several different types of investors, as shown in Fig. 3.12. These include 30 public pension funds, 25 foundations or endowments, 11 banks or financial services firms, nine investment firms, nine government-related investment organizations, seven asset management companies, five sovereign wealth funds, four private pension funds, three insurance companies, three corporates, two family offices, two fund of funds managers, and one advisor. Their headquarters are mainly in North America (58) and Western Europe (30). The Asia-Pacific region and the Middle East and Africa count eight and ten funds, respectively. One other LP is based in Latin America and none is based in Central or Eastern Europe.

**Table 3.3** Agritech investors, as of the end of December 2021

| | Obs. | Mean | St. Dev. | Min | Median | Max |
|---|---|---|---|---|---|---|
| Number of fund commitments | 111 | 3.75 | 4.58 | 1 | 2 | 29 |
| Allocation to alternatives (%) | 66 | 26.54 | 14.03 | 0.02 | 26.2 | 56.5 |
| Allocation infrastructure (%) | 18 | 5.01 | 4.09 | 0.4 | 4.08 | 13.6 |
| AUM ($ million) | 22 | 86,173 | 194,046 | 171 | 23,220 | 912,987 |
| Total active investments | 15 | 96.00 | 125.33 | 1 | 55 | 488 |
| Min bite size ($ million) | 12 | 9 | 19 | 0 | 1 | 67 |
| Max bite size ($ million) | 14 | 320 | 484 | 1 | 80 | 1685 |

Source: authors' elaboration of data provided by Agri Investor and Capital IQ Pro

According to the information available on their corresponding tearsheets provided by Agri Investor, most of these LPs (101) indicate agribusiness as one of their preferred target sectors, together with farmland (38), timber/forestland (38), and water (30). Then, 96 out of these 111 LPs explicitly list agritech among their favorite allocation strategies in the agriculture investment space.

To get a clearer picture of the variety of their approaches to agritech investing and their different investment styles, for the LPs in our sample we collected additional information from Capital IQ Pro. More specifically, for each one, we merged the information obtained from their tearsheets on Agri Investor with additional data available in the company reports on the Capital IQ Pro platform, based on individual text searches of their names. Table 3.3 reports a summary of descriptive statistics for the LPs in our sample, which we take as representative of the agritech investor universe, as of the end of December 2021.

On average, our LPs have committed capital to more than three different funds, with a maximum of 29. This suggests that the agritech investment space is populated by mid-sized and large investors with long track records. Alternative asset classes have an important role in their portfolios. The average allocation to alternatives is over 26.5% and can be as much as 56.5%. Infrastructure contributes substantially to the share of their capital directed to alternatives. More precisely, the LPs in our sample allocate on average about 5% of their commitments to the infrastructure asset class. The number of active investments per LP is on average 96, reflecting the typically small average bite size of agritech investments, which as far as mean value range from a minimum of $9 to a maximum of $320 million.

Only six out of the LPs in our sample of agritech investors are also ranked among the world's top 50 infrastructure investors in the annual list prepared by Infrastructure Investor, based on the market value of investors' private infrastructure investment portfolios both through third-party managed investment vehicles and direct investments.[6] To conduct a more in-depth investigation of the degree to which the agritech investor universe overlaps with infrastructure, we also collected more

[6]The list compiled by Infrastructure Investor of the 50 largest infrastructure investors globally by market value of their infrastructure investment portfolios is available on its web page (http://www.infrastructureinvestor.com)

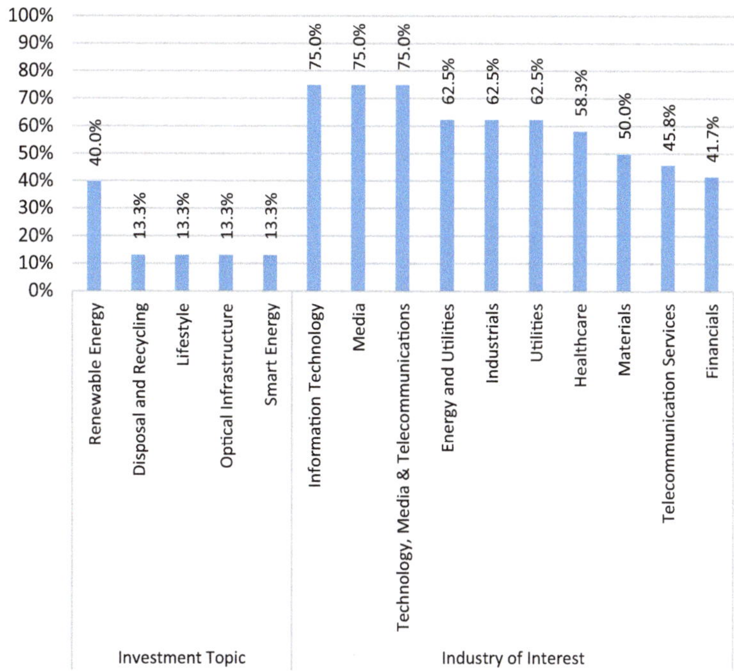


**Fig. 3.13** Investment styles of agritech investors: topics and industries of interest (Source: authors' elaboration of data provided by Capital IQ Pro)

qualitative information from Capital IQ Pro on LPs' investment topics and industries of interest, as well as their preferred deal structure type and development stage.

As with the GPs, this information allows us to classify LPs across a number of non-mutually exclusive categories based on their investment preferences. Figure 3.13 shows the resulting top five recurrent investment topics as well as the top ten industries of interest among the LPs in our sample. We note that the most frequently recurring investment topics among agritech-focused investors include renewable energy (40.0%), optical infrastructure (13.3%), smart energy (13.3%), disposal and recycling (13.3%), and lifestyle (13.3%), which are all some of the typical targets of infrastructure investors. Nonetheless, the LPs in our sample report interest in investment opportunities across a broad spectrum of industries. Consistent with a generalist approach, a majority of them cover many of the major business activities, including industrials (62.5%), energy and utilities (62.5%), healthcare (58.3%), materials (50%), and financials (41.7%). However, their dominant focus seems to be trained on information technologies, media, and telecom (75%).

The investment preferences of the LPs in our sample, as regards deal structure and development stage, are reported in Fig. 3.14. The dominant focus in terms of the first is on buyout (73.9%) and growth capital (56.5%) strategies. Other structures are much less frequent. Fewer LPs target deals related to recapitalization (25%), private investments in public equity (8.7%), industry consolidation (11.5%), or mezzanine

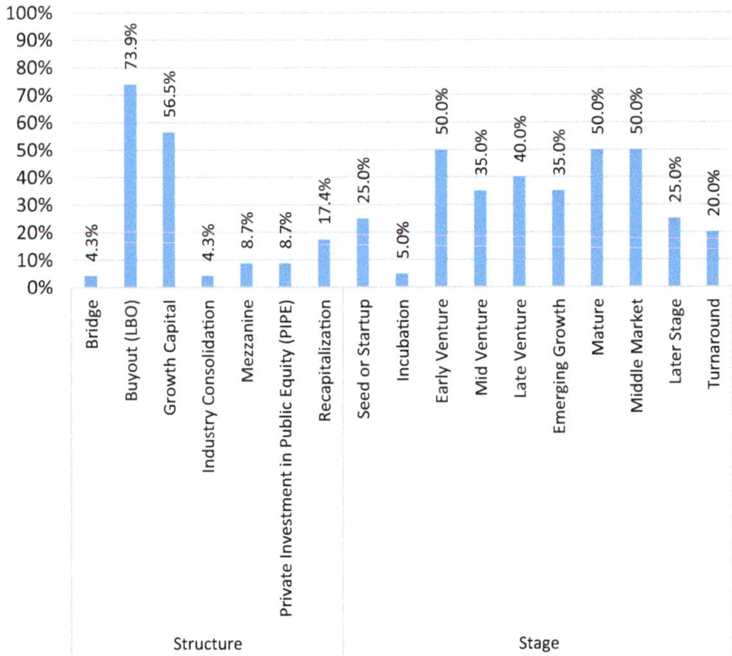


**Fig. 3.14** Investment styles of agritech investors: deal structure and development stage (Source: authors' elaboration of data provided by Capital IQ Pro)

(8.7%) and bridge (4.3%) finance. Moreover, early ventures as well as mature and middle market companies are the preferred targets for one of every two LPs in our sample. These are followed by companies that are in the late venture (40%), mid venture (35%), emerging growth (35%) seed or startup (25%), later stage (25%), or turnaround (20%). Only a few of the LPs in our sample favor the incubation stage (5%).

Figure 3.15 shows instead the frequency with which the agritech-focused LPs in our sample indicate interest in infrastructure-related investment topics or industries. As in our analysis of GPs, we tag each investment topic or industry of interest reported by the LPs in our sample that is related to renewable or conventional energy, telecoms, transport, utilities, social, and other infrastructure. Also in this case, the vast majority of the LPs in our sample (80%) indicate interest in infrastructure-related investment topics, especially those concerned with renewable energy (46.7%) but also in the sphere of social infrastructure (20%), transport (6.7%), and telecoms (6.7%). The interest in infrastructure-related industries is even more generalized, almost all the LPs in our sample (91.7%) report targeting industries related to telecoms (79.2%), utilities (62.5%), social (62.5%), and other (20.8%) infrastructure services, as well as renewable (37.5%) or conventional (33.3%) energy, and transport (25%). This is once again consistent with a substantial overlap between agritech-focused LPs and the broader pool of investors in the

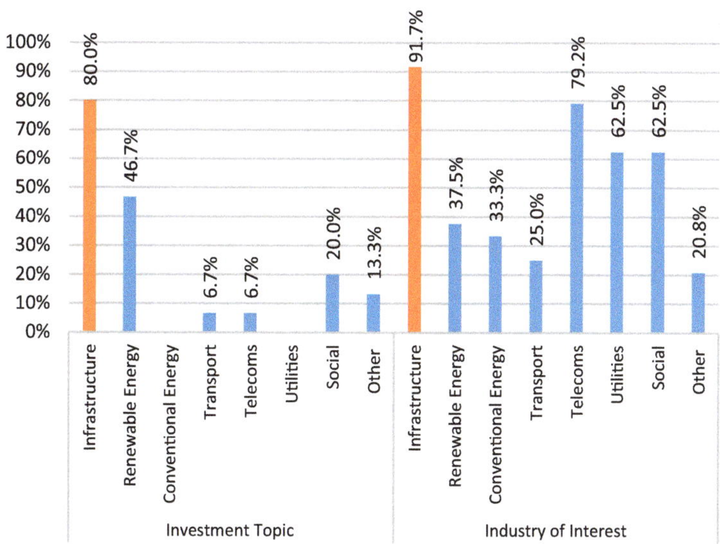


**Fig. 3.15** Agritech investor interest in infrastructure-related investment topics and industries (Source: authors' elaboration of data provided by Capital IQ Pro)

infrastructure investment space, confirming the potential of agritech to emerge as one of the most prominent investment themes within the infrastructure asset class.

## Transactions and Target Companies

We conclude our investigation of the agritech investment space by taking a closer look at recent transactions, with a focus on the pool of target companies. The objective is to provide interested investors with an initial approximation of the investment opportunity set and an early assessment of possible infrastructure plays.

Figure 3.16 shows the recent evolution of transaction volumes in upstream agritech between 2018 and 2021, according to data compiled by AgFunder (2022), both in aggregate deal dollar value (left-hand panel) and deal count (right-hand panel). Deal volume has been consistently on the rise since 2018. More specifically we observe an almost threefold upsurge in the aggregate value of deals in the last four years, from $6.9 billion in 2018 to $19.7 billion in 2021. Analogously, the number of deals has more than doubled, from 824 in 2018 to 1827. Consistent with the emerging nature of the asset class, deal size is still very small on average, about $10 million in 2021, but it is on the rise year by year.

These transactions include several different upstream agritech applications, categorized as summarized in Table 3.4.

Figure 3.17 breaks down transaction volumes between 2018 and 2021 across different agritech upstream applications, both in terms of aggregate deal dollar value (top panel) and deal count (bottom panel). Consistent with a rising interest in the

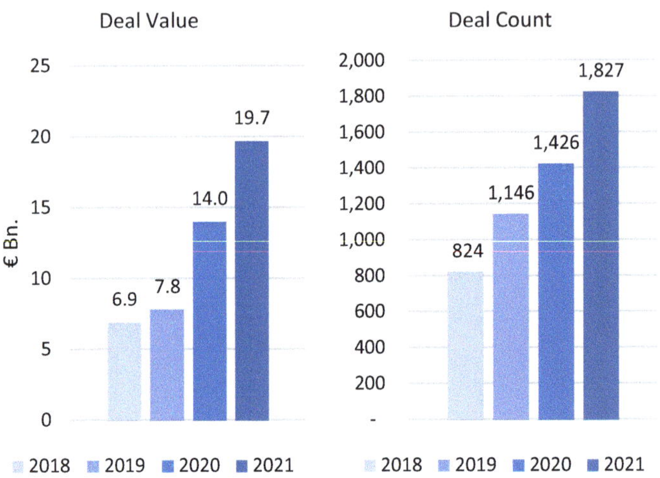


**Fig. 3.16** Agritech transaction volumes, 2018–2021 (Source: authors' elaboration of data provided by AgFunder)

**Table 3.4** Upstream agritech applications

| Application | Examples |
|---|---|
| Biotechnology | On-farm inputs for crops and animal agriculture, including genetics, biomedicine, breeding, and animal health |
| Agribusiness Marketplace | Commodities trading platforms, online input procurement, equipment leasing |
| Biomaterials and Bioenergy | Non-food extraction and processing, feedstock technology, cannabis, and pharmaceuticals |
| Innovative Food | Cultured meat, novel ingredients, plant-based proteins |
| Farm Management Software, Sensing & IoT | Agriculture data capturing devices, decision support software, big data analytics |
| Farm Robotics | On-farm machinery, automation, drone manufacturers, growth equipment |
| Midstream Technologies | Food safety and traceability technologies, logistics and transport, processing technologies |
| Novel Farming Systems | Indoor farms, aquaculture, insect and algae production |
| Miscellaneous | Fintech for farmers |

Source: AgFunder

asset class from different types of investors, transaction volume is on the rise for all different agritech applications. The largest contributions in terms of deal dollar value and deal count come from transactions related to innovative foods (424 deals for €4.8 bn.) and midstream technology (382 deals for €3.8 bn.). These are followed by biotechnologies (209 deals for $2.1 bn.), biomaterials and bioenergy applications (172 deals for €2.6 bn.), together with novel farming systems (171 deals for €2.3 bn.). The remaining deal volume is made up of transactions in the agribusiness marketplace (110 deals for €1.3 bn.), farm management systems (161 deals for €1.2

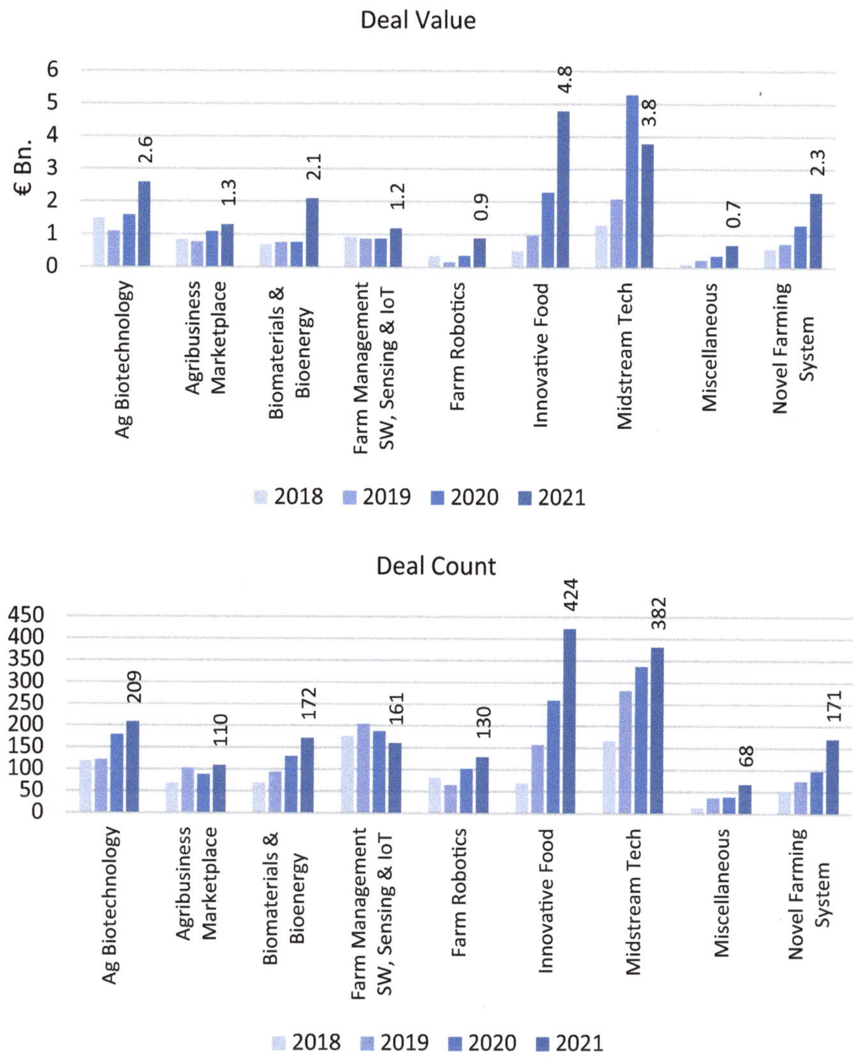


**Fig. 3.17** Agritech transaction volumes by target application, 2018–2021 (Source: authors' elaboration of data provided by AgFunder)

bn.), farm robotics (130 deals for €0.9 bn.), and miscellaneous (68 deals for €0.7 bn.). The average deal size ranges across different agritech applications from slightly less than $7 million in farm robotics to $13.4 million in novel farming systems.

Considering that infrastructure investors typically prefer larger bite sizes, we conducted our analysis of the agritech investment opportunity set focusing only on the 15 largest transactions each year. More specifically, for every agritech application we identify the targets of the 15 largest transactions each year from the

**Table 3.5** Target companies in agritech transactions: summary statistics

| | Obs. | Mean | St. Dev. | Min | Median | Max |
|---|---|---|---|---|---|---|
| Latest round number | 279 | 4.65 | 3.02 | 1 | 4 | 18 |
| Latest round size ($ million) | 243 | 63.86 | 86.14 | 0 | 32 | 575 |
| Total raised ($ million) | 275 | 135.27 | 237.81 | 0 | 59 | 2896 |
| Age | 240 | 8.94 | 6.80 | 2 | 7 | 55 |

Source: authors' elaboration of data provided by Capital IQ Pro

AgFunder annual investment reports.[7] This brings down the number of deals in our sample to 471, for a total of 323 target companies. We then run individual searches for each one of these target firms on Capital IQ Pro, to collect additional qualitative and quantitative information useful to profile them.

Table 3.5 provides some summary statistics on the size of these targets. These are typically recently incorporated companies. The average target is only about nine years old, and the median one is two years younger. Indeed, only about one out of five targets in our sample was incorporated before 2009. Many of these companies have already gone through multiple rounds of financing (more than four on average) and some of them have raised significant amounts of capital. The average target raised about $64 million in the last round and more than $135 overall. The largest round size is $575 million and the total amount raised by the largest target is almost $3 billion. Therefore, in the higher end of our sample there are indeed companies that could fit the investment criteria well and appear on the radar of mid- and large-sized infrastructure investors.

Moreover, Fig. 3.18 provides an overview of their stage of development. Consistent with their recent incorporation, the majority of the targets in our samples are still in their early venture status, mostly going through their first rounds of financing (i.e., Series A, 12%; Series B, 23%; and Series C, 13%).

On a more qualitative stance, Capital IQ Pro further classifies companies based on their primary industries, topic tags, and Crunchbase categories. Similar to the analysis of GPs and LPs, we use this information to identify the most recurrent target industries, topic tags, and Crunchbase categories within the agritech investment opportunity set. We also indicate where the points of intersection are with the infrastructure asset class.

Figure 3.19 reports the ten most recurrent target industries. We observe that the agritech investment opportunity set comprises a diverse group of industries. The largest concentrations of target companies are in biotechnology (13.6%), packaged foods and meats (13%), agricultural products (8.4%), internet software and services (8.4%), application software (7.1%), electronic equipment and instruments (6.8%), agricultural and farm equipment (5.3%), commodity chemicals (2.8%), internet and direct marketing retail (2.5%), and pharmaceuticals (2.2%). Based on EDHECinfra's infrastructure taxonomy we are able to link only about 11% of the targets in our

[7]The information is extracted form AgFunder (2018, 2019, 2020, 2021a, 2021b, 2022).

**Fig. 3.18** Target companies in agritech transactions: stage of development (Source: authors' elaboration of data provided by Capital IQ Pro)

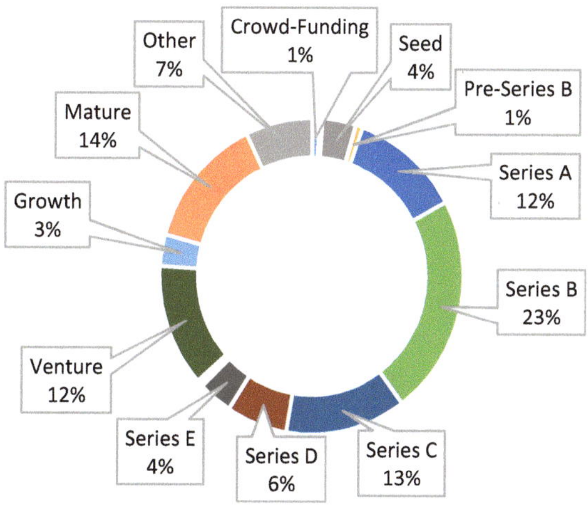


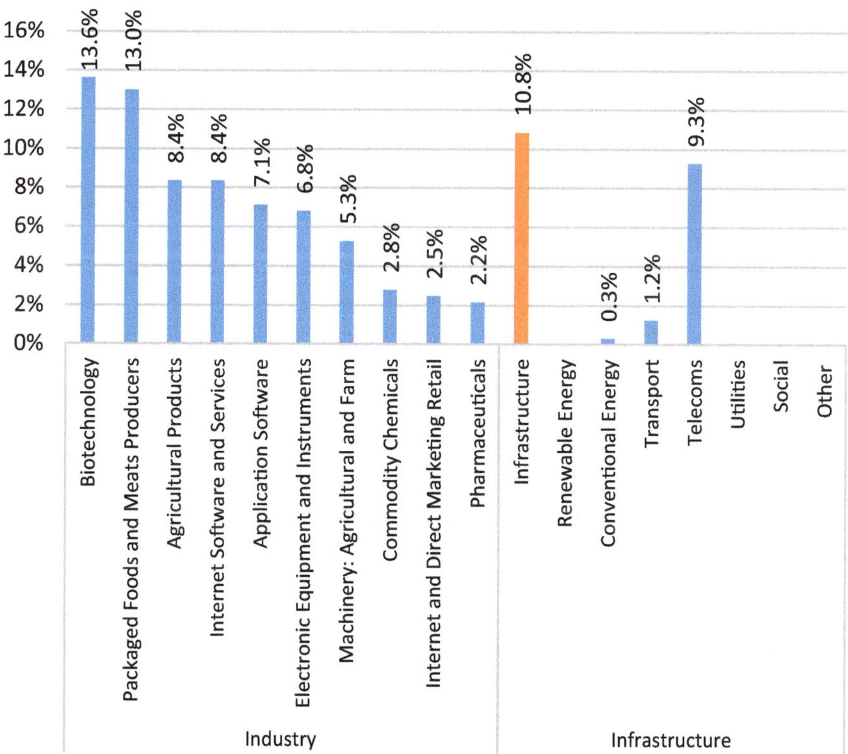


**Fig. 3.19** Target companies in agritech transactions: top ten industries (Source: authors' elaboration of data provided by Capital IQ Pro)

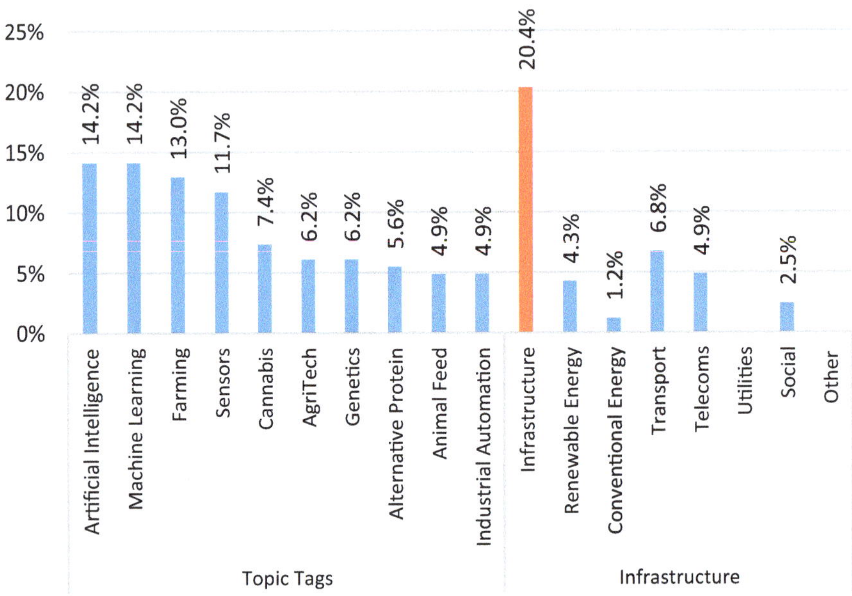


**Fig. 3.20** Target companies in agritech transactions: top ten topic tags (Source: authors elaboration of data provided by Capital IQ Pro)

sample to the industries typically associated with the infrastructure asset class, most of them in telecoms (9.3%).

Then we conducted the same analysis on the basis of non-mutually exclusive topic tags, which provide a finer categorization of target companies. Figure 3.20 reports the ten most recurrent topic tags and the incidence of the infrastructure-related ones. Among the agritech-focused target companies in our sample, we found artificial intelligence (14.2%), machine learning (14.2%), farming (13%), sensors (11.7%), chemicals (7.4%), agritech (6.2%), genetics (6.2%), alternative protein (5.6%), animal feed (4.9%), and industrial automation (4.9%). In this case, we are able to link about 20% of the targets in our sample to topic tags potentially associated with the infrastructure asset class. A majority of them are related to transport (6.8%), telecoms (4.9%), and renewable energy (4.3%).

A very similar picture emerges when we analyze Crunchbase categories, which provide an even sharper classification of companies. Figure 3.21 reports the ten most recurrent categories and the relative incidence of the infrastructure-related ones. Among the agritech-focused target companies in our sample, there is agriculture (33.9%), biotechnology (23.6%), farming (20.7%), food and beverage (19.2), agritech (15.5%), software (15.1%), robotics (11.4%), artificial intelligence (10.7%), food processing (10.3%), and the internet (8.1%). We are able to link about 30% of the targets in our sample to categories potentially associated with the infrastructure asset class. A majority of them are related to transport (12.9%), telecoms (11.4%), and renewable energy (6.6%).

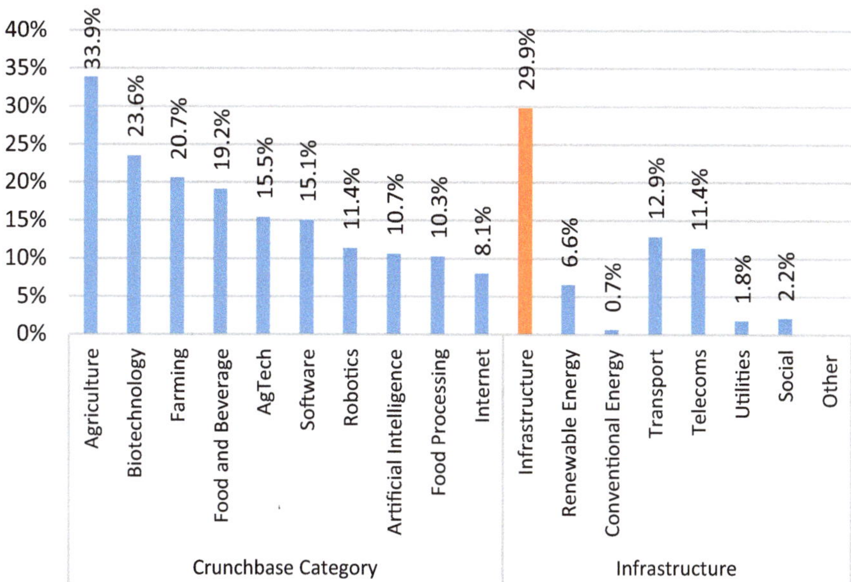


**Fig. 3.21** Target companies in agritech transactions: top ten Crunchbase categories (Source: authors' elaboration of data provided by Capital IQ Pro)

Overall, our analysis seems to suggest therefore that there is a considerable area of overlap between the agritech investment opportunity set and the infrastructure investment space. More specifically, our analysis of target companies confirms that investment opportunities fitting the investment criteria of infrastructure investors can be found at the intersection of agritech with transport, telecoms, and renewable energy.

## 3.4 Conclusion

This chapter poses salient questions to investors and asset managers about the convergence of contiguous asset classes in the alternative assets investment space. In particular, we look at the intersection between agriculture and infrastructure and investigate the prospects for investors and asset managers with a long-term horizon, such as those who are investing in infrastructure, to embrace a theme investing approach focused on agritech.

The picture that emerges from our analysis of the agritech investment space indicates that:

- The agritech investor base is largely overlapping with that of infrastructure. The vast majority of the LPs in our sample are ready to commit funds across multiple segments within the alternatives asset class.

- Most asset managers have a generalist approach, which puts them in the ideal position to facilitate investor mobility, crossing the boundaries between different segments of alternative investments, and allowing them to embrace a more flexible investment approach and to position themselves to exploit the long-term strategic opportunities that are emerging in agriculture.
- The agritech investment opportunity set partly intersects with that of infrastructure. In particular, infrastructure investors can find interesting investment opportunities in agritech applications related to transport, telecoms, and renewable energy. Their focus will be only on the larger companies in their late stages of development.

Based on the results of our analysis, we expect that under the pressure of social and technological trends, the boundaries between infrastructure and agriculture will blur even further. In fact, we will see more agritech companies reach critical size and stage of development to appear on the radars of infrastructure investors and asset managers.

All this means that both infrastructure investors and asset managers need to get ready for the transformative changes ahead by strategically adjusting their investment processes to identify the most promising agritech applications within their sectors of expertise. For example, we recommend focusing on new technologies in telecoms that can improve agriculture productivity and food management, innovations in renewable energy that will allow more efficient and sustainable use of resources, on new advancements in transportation that will enhance food security and consolidate/shorten the product supply chain.

## References

AgFunder. (2018). *Agri-FoodTech investing report*. https://agfunder.com/research/agrifood-tech-investing-report-2018/

AgFunder. (2019). *Agri-FoodTech investing report*. https://agfunder.com/research/agfunder-agrifood-tech-investing-report-2019/

AgFunder. (2020). *FarmTech investment report*. https://agfunder.com/research/2020-farm-tech-investment-report/

AgFunder. (2021a). *Agri-FoodTech investment report*. https://agfunder.com/research/2021-AgFunder-agrifoodtech-investment-report/

AgFunder. (2021b). *FarmTech investment report*. https://agfunder.com/research/2021-farm-tech-investment-report/

AgFunder. (2022). *Agri-FoodTech investment report*. https://agfunder.com/research/2022-agfunder-agrifoodtech-investment-report/

Alliance Bernstein. (2010). *Deflating inflation: Redefining the inflation-resistant portfolio*. April 2010 https://www.alliancebernstein.com/CmsObjectABD/PDF/Research_WhitePaper/RWP_DeflationInflationBlackbook.pdf

EDHECinfra. (2022). *The Infrastructure Company Classification Standard (TICCS)*. 2022 Edition. https://edhec.infrastructure.institute/ticcs/

Gatti, S., & Chiarella, C. (2020). *Disruption in the infrastructure sector challenges and opportunities for developers, investors and asset managers*. Springer. https://doi.org/10.1007/978-3-030-44667-3

IPE Real Assets. (2019). *Agriculture: Germ of an asset class*. July/August 2019. https://realassets.ipe.com/agriculture-germ-of-an-asset-class/10032037.article

Preqin. (2016). *Special report: Agriculture*. September 2016. https://docs.preqin.com/reports/Preqin-Special-Report-Agriculture-September-2016.pdf

Preqin. (2017). *Overview of the agriculture industry*. April 2017. https://www.preqin.com/insights/research/factsheets/overview-of-the-agriculture-industry

Preqin. (2022a). *Investor Outlook: Alternative Assets H2 2022*. https://www.preqin.com/insights/research/investor-outlooks/preqin-investor-outlook-alternative-assets-h2-2022

Preqin. (2022b). *Quarterly update: Infrastructure Q2 2022*. https://www.preqin.com/insights/research/quarterly-updates/infrastructure-q2-2022

Preqin. (2022c). *Quarterly update: Natural resources Q2 2022*. https://www.preqin.com/insights/research/quarterly-updates/natural-resources-q2-2022

Preqin. (2022d). *Alternatives in 2022*. https://www.preqin.com/insights/research/reports/alternatives-in-2022

Preqin. (2022e). *Global natural resources report*. https://www.preqin.com/insights/global-reports/2022-preqin-global-natural-resources-report

Preqin. (2022f). *Global infrastructure report*. https://www.preqin.com/insights/global-reports/2022-preqin-global-infrastructure-report

Sherrick, B. (2020). *The relationship between inflation and farmland returns*. TIAA Center for Farmland Research. https://farmland.illinois.edu/wp-content/uploads/2020/10/Relationship-between-inflation-and-farmland-returns.pdf

UBS. (2020). *The last, great untapped asset class*. https://irei.com/wp-content/uploads/2020/12/Jan-2021-UBSAssetManagement-SponsorReport.pdf

# Conclusions

Stefano Gatti, Vitaliano Fiorillo, and Carlo Chiarella
ANTIN IP Professor of Infrastructure Finance, Department of Finance, Bocconi University, Milan, Italy
AGRI Lab, SDA Bocconi School of Management, Bocconi University, Milan, Italy
Department of Finance and Accounting, CUNEF Universidad, Madrid, Spain

The contributions in this book provide very specific insights for the future of agriculture, highlighting the key challenges for the sector and the innovations that are underway. The findings of the authors have clear implications for incumbents, disruptors, regulators, policymakers, investors, and asset managers. This final section summarizes the results of the various analyses conducted in the previous chapters, highlighting the key outcomes and connecting them in a unified framework from the standpoint of infrastructure investors and asset managers.

For these stakeholders three key takeaways emerge.

First, the analysis in Chap. 1 provides fundamental insights into the long-term changes that the sector will experience in the next few years. More in detail, it points out global megatrends that are already affecting human production and consumption models, and that will have a more and more direct impact on the agriculture value chain in the near future. The most influential driving forces include climate change and resource scarcity, growing demand and changing dietary preferences (also deriving from evolving income levels), technological innovation and hyperconnectivity, and integration of global trade. However, many other forces of change are at work at a broader level: big data proliferation and ubiquity, generational dynamics derived from demographic trends, and the need for new job skills are surely among them. These have the potential to impact the agribusiness industry, like every other aspect of human life.

Given the complexity of the current production and consumption models as well as natural ecosystems, effective solutions to tackle such challenges must acknowledge their interconnectedness. Crucially, the analysis in Chap. 1 also shows that all these forces interact one with another, with reinforcing or mitigating effects. From



S. Gatti et al. (eds.), *Agriculture as an Alternative Investment*, Contributions to Finance and Accounting, https://doi.org/10.1007/978-3-031-27918-8

the point of view of investors and asset managers, a clear understanding of these forces is essential to identify the best investment opportunities and to design lasting and sustainable investment strategies, adapted to a changing investment environment.

In some ways, the results of the multi-perspective interdisciplinary analysis conducted in this chapter show a slightly different picture of innovations and technologies when seen from the "money talks" perspective that we find in several reports on agritech investments. While these reports show a polarization of investments downstream in the value chain, the latter being the hotspot of investments from the pandemic onward, the chapter shows that true novelties, those with the highest potential for an adaptation strategy within the context of the key driving forces, lie at the other end. The picture that emerges from the analysis of innovations in the agribusiness industry indicates specifically that they are lacking among retailers, but there is a concentration of technological innovations upstream, among the suppliers of technological solutions and input providers. All the innovations analyzed here, except for food delivery (the downstream hotspot that now looks like it's failing to live up to investors' hopes of returns [1]), respond to one or more of the following objectives: (i) to reduce the impact of human activities on the environment; (ii) to boost agriculture productivity; (iii) to curtail food loss and waste; (iv) to shore up agriculture resilience to climate change; and (v) to increase food safety. These objectives can all be traced back to the four main challenges affecting the agribusiness industry as delineated in the chapter.

Second, the analysis in Chap. 2 identifies a large set of promising investable applications and maps them in terms of potential interest for infrastructure investors and asset managers. While some still belong to the world of pure venture capital and startups, others can already represent interesting investment opportunities for infrastructure-oriented investors. Among them, technologies that aim to revamp current models to adapt to ongoing transformations are the most promising. Thus, from the point of view of investors and asset managers, adaptability must be the keyword for the near future, and the technologies that encourage this approach must be the primary focus. We refer in particular to investing in products and processes that, with the introduction of new technologies, aim to:

- improve agriculture productivity and the management of food loss and waste;
- make more efficient and sustainable use of resources; and,
- enhance food security and consolidate/shorten the product supply chain.

More specifically, another interesting conclusion to be drawn from the analysis in this chapter is that innovation in the agribusiness industry is driven by viable businesses and technologies that have already successfully entered the market.

(although they are still subject to continuous upgrades). Invention-level innovations, technically at a proof-of-concept stage, are rarer and tend to represent a branch

[1]Morgan Stanley, 2022, "Can Food Delivery Apps Deliver Profits for Investors?" https://www.morganstanley.com/ideas/food-delivery-app-profits, last accessed: Nov 14, 2022.

of technologies and know-how already developed in other sectors and/or businesses rather than an agribusiness/challenge-specific solution.

A clear example is vertical farming, where innovation lies in the architecture of often mature technologies and the turning point seems to be the cost of energy. Current studies focus mainly on LED advancement, as illumination accounts for the biggest cost item for vertical farms.

Other crucial fields of research in vertical farming include species-specific plant treatments and internal logistics optimization. Nonetheless, market operators are very interested in this business due to its characteristics of continued availability and full traceability of products. Moreover, pharmaceutical and cosmetic industries represent potential markets for vertical farm produce. Several other technologies not representing a large enough improvement per se still may be attractive for investments if focused on technological advancements that aim to reduce the final cost of products or services.

Third, the analysis in Chap. 3 confirms that the very concept of infrastructure investing can be stretched to embrace agriculture investments to innovate the technological processes used in agriculture and farming; the focus here is to provide the right balance between reliable income streams and capital appreciation/capital gains. More in detail, the analysis of agritech-focused private equity and the venture capital space shows that asset managers and investors are increasingly embracing a theme-based investing approach and positioning themselves to exploit the long-term strategic opportunities that are emerging in agriculture. Indeed, the agritech investor base largely overlaps with the infrastructure one; most asset managers have a generalist approach, and the agritech investment opportunity set partly intersects with that of infrastructure. In particular, even if many potential targets still struggle to meet their size and stage of development criteria, infrastructure investors can find interesting investment opportunities in agritech applications within their sectors of expertise—namely, transport, telecoms, and renewable energy.

Looking ahead, investors and asset managers must recognize that all technological trends and applications analyzed here are expected to grow in the coming years, especially as the industry challenges they address will become increasingly urgent. Sustainability, in particular, is at the core of any further development of the industry, being not only a valuable leverage for businesses to gain a competitive advantage, but also a necessary approach for them to survive in the market.

However, the outlook is not free of challenges. Success is still dependent on different factors that are mainly contingent on further technological and scientific advances to enhance efficiency and reduce costs, the design of innovative business models to enable large-scale deployment, normative support, and the acceptance of value-chain operators and consumers. From a stakeholder perspective, despite the fascinating side of some ground-breaking applications and technologies, consumer and industry operator legitimacy together with a conducive and stable regulatory framework are crucial to support the diffusion of innovations and allow their potential to be unleashed effectively against global challenges. Without such elements, technological innovations' large-scale deployment could be hindered and/or end up being impossible, regardless of their potential.

In this respect, politics is a variable to consider. The risk is that its improvised, blanket solutions may not always adequately take into account national, business, and environmental specificities, for example in the case of Europe. Moreover, the need for a mindset change, especially on farms, which are at the core of our future possibility of creating a sustainable agribusiness system, must not be underestimated. Although some new human capital is indeed coming from other industries and backgrounds, the agribusiness industry evolution must necessarily involve traditional farmers. This requires a mindset change, which can be only partially triggered by generational dynamics. Analogously, consumers must be given time to get used to drastic changes and accept new technologies that will transform production and their consumption habits in ways considered impossible a few years ago—for example, insect farming, vertical farms, or cultivated food.

Accordingly, four main clusters of innovation emerge from the analysis:

- Technologies expected to proliferate but still struggling for full-scale adoption of their most advanced versions (aquaculture, agrovoltaics, packaging, and agritech). Investment, in this case, should address overcoming scale cost challenges in some circumstances, and increasing stakeholder acceptance.
- Technologies with potential for diffusion but ethically opposed by different groups of stakeholders or lacking a normative framework (alternative proteins, food preservation techniques, insect farming, vegetal NBTs). For such technologies, investments in some countries may be more risky than others. For example, where milk/meat farmers still represent a significant special interest group, alternative proteins may be banned for political reasons. Some of the technologies in this cluster, though, have the highest potential to counter the effects of climate change and/or restore an ecosystem balance.
- Technologies expected to be more commonly adopted if operating costs can be reduced (livestock NBTs, desalination, vertical farming). In this cluster, investments should focus on process improvement and research and/or operating cost reduction.
- Dependent technologies whose potential is tightly connected to the adoption rate of other supporting technologies (bioenergy, algae culture, fish NBTs, food delivery). The future of algae culture, for example, is linked to the success of alternative technologies. The diffusion of biofuels derived from algae might be hindered by public subsidies for electric vehicles. Similarly, the adoption of biomass-based biofuels will be influenced by the applicability of hydrogen and batteries. Investment-wise, such technologies have to be considered as part of a complementary portfolio.

Last but not least, we ought to point out that it's not just about technologies; it's also a matter of production systems that need to evolve, taking into consideration our renewed understanding of natural ecosystems and the value of the services that they provide, and which we need to maintain, restore, and improve through our actions. Therefore, from an innovation management standpoint, there are two main implications for investors and asset managers. The first conclusion is that technologies and novelties should be analyzed by looking at a system-wide picture of the future. As noted in Chap. 2, Section 1.1, the development and diffusion of technological innovations in a society cannot be explained simply by looking at individual firms or unique technologies. Novel technologies, especially when they clash with established social rules and practices and differ considerably from dominant technologies, face difficulties in market uptake due to strong skepticism and a lack of societal legitimacy.

The second conclusion regards the need to clearly understand the concept of system change when it comes to agribusiness. The underlying awareness of a global agricultural system threatened by climate change will probably move investors more and more toward a different set of indicators to evaluate opportunities and asset allocation. Regardless of technological advancements, agribusiness draws attention to natural capital. The pressure from climate change that agribusiness is exposed to is now a matter of how the available natural capital has been managed so far. Technologies and techniques applied in agriculture for over a century are now failing to counter the effects of climate change, on the one hand, and seem to have a low adaptation rate, on the other. Investing in agribusiness is all about changing this paradigm.

MIX
Papier aus verantwortungsvollen Quellen
Paper from responsible sources
FSC® C105338

If you have any concerns about our products, you can contact us on
**ProductSafety@springernature.com**

In case Publisher is established outside the EU, the EU authorized representative is:
**Springer Nature Customer Service Center GmbH**
**Europaplatz 3, 69115 Heidelberg, Germany**

Printed by Libri Plureos GmbH
in Hamburg, Germany